postmodernism

a beginner's guide

postmodernism

a beginner's guide

kevin hart

ONEWORLD

OXFORD

For Gail Ward

postmodernism: a beginner's guide

Oneworld Publications
(Sales and Editorial)
185 Banbury Road
Oxford OX2 7AR
England
www.oneworld-publications.com

© Kevin Hart, 2004

ISBN 1–85168–338–0

Cover design by the Bridgewater Book Company
Typeset by Jayvee, Trivandrum, India
Printed and bound by Thomson Press (India) Ltd

contents

overview

chapter one – postmodernism: some guides

We begin by going on a tour in which some leading figures of post-modernism are introduced: Jean-François Lyotard, Jacques Lacan, Jacques Derrida, Gilles Deleuze, Félix Guattari and Michel Foucault. Some important distinctions are made: *postmodernism* is distinguished from *modernism*, then from *postmodernity*, and finally from *post-structuralism*. Three other important words are discussed: *post-humanist*, *post-metaphysical* and *avant garde*.

chapter two – the loss of origin

Try as one might postmodernism cannot be reduced to a viewpoint or even a small collection of viewpoints. However, it can be clarified by examining three widely held theories: *anti-essentialism*, *anti-realism* and *anti-foundationalism*. Each of these is discussed, and the last one is treated in detail. Arguments against firm foundations in knowledge go back to the ancient Greeks, though postmodernists take their bearings from the declaration of Friedrich Nietzsche's madman, 'God is dead'. What this means, and how it relates to *nihilism* and *perspectivism*, is discussed. Derrida's anti-foundationalism is contrasted with Richard Rorty's. Yet anti-foundationalism is hardly the preserve of 'postmodern' thinkers, as they are usually grouped: it is also an important part of analytic philosophy. Brief introductions are made to Wilfred Sellars, Willard van Orman Quine and Donald Davidson. Why do we think of the European anti-foundationalists as postmodern, and not the Americans?

chapter three – postmodern experience

Do we postmoderns have different experiences from those that our parents and grandparents had? Or does postmodernity tell us something new and distinctive about experience? Talk about the postmodern begins by an appeal to experience, while experience is a theme of postmodern talk. Maurice Blanchot is taken as a guide to 'experience' in postmodern times, and particular attention is given to his notion of the experience of the outside. Many postmodernists have learned from Blanchot, especially from his idea of living an event as image. Baudrillard is one, as his notion of the hyper-real suggests. His treatment of the 1991 Gulf War is considered. In some respects the world of tele-technology and digital information is a world at the end of history. The idea is considered by way of Derrida's reading of Marx, Kojève and Fukuyama.

chapter four – the fragmentary

The Romantics were drawn to the fragment; and postmodernists, who distance themselves from Romanticism, affirm the fragmentary. The notion of the fragmentary is introduced by way of Walter Benjamin and Jewish mysticism, and then clarified by Blanchot. Postmodernists often object to totality or unity, but what exactly is their objection to it? The ethics of Emmanuel Lévinas, who values infinity over totality, are introduced, and the notion of 'relation without relation' explained. Luce Irigaray's work on sexual difference is considered. Is Christianity related to unity, as Blanchot suggests? Or can it be thought by way of the fragmentary?

chapter five – the postmodern bible

Does postmodernism reject the Bible, the bastion of unity and transcendent truth, or does it reinterpret it to its own ends? Whether the Bible forms a whole, or even a grand narrative, is considered. The idea of a 'postmodern Bible' is assessed, and is followed by a discussion of Harold Bloom's understanding of J. What does the Bible bequeath us? Dialogue, Blanchot insists; and a discussion of this claim leads us to consider the prayer 'Come' to the Messiah. It is something that intrigues Derrida, whose biblical interpretations are briefly analyzed, and whose views on theology are introduced.

chapter six – postmodern religion

Religion in postmodern times is distinguished from postmodern religion. On the one hand, fundamentalism is the postmodern inter-pretation of religion and, on the other hand, postmodern religion elaborates itself by way of one or more liberalisms. In Christianity today we might distinguish a/theology and radical orthodoxy. Somewhere between these extremes we can discern a deconstruction of Christianity. Various understandings of this are considered, and special attention is given to Derrida's take on 'negative theology' and prayer. Is Derrida right to figure the other person as other than me in each and every way, and therefore to be akin to God? Special attention is given to Derrida's reading of Abraham's sacrifice of Isaac, and to his notion of 'religion without religion'.

chapter seven – the gift: a debate

Is postmodernity secular or does the postmodern render possible a critique of secularism? The question alerts us, once again, to the plurality at the heart of postmodernity. George Lindbeck's post-liberal theology is briefly considered, along with Hans Urs von Balthasar's understanding of theology at the end of modernity and Karl Rahner's mysticism of everyday life. Two thinkers who look to von Balthasar are then discussed in detail: Jean-Luc Marion and John Milbank, and they are examined in the light of their analysis of a theme that is at the forefront of contemporary debate in postmodernism: the gift.

conclusion – guides and another guide

Other possible topics in postmodernism are raised, including psychoanalysis and politics. Critical realism and eco-criticism are flagged as important challenges to postmodernism.

author's note

This book is an introduction to postmodernism for people who know little or nothing about it. Special interest is taken in the questions of how religion stands in the postmodern world and how postmodernism stands before religion. In the spirit of the series of which it is a part, I have not quoted any author or supplied any endnotes. I regard this primer as a contribution to teaching, not research, and I wrote it as though imagining I was giving a series of general talks to undergraduates and other interested people. When you have finished reading the book, make a photocopy of the bibliography and then give the book to a friend. If these chapters have any value, it will be in leading you to read works by the people whose ideas I introduce and sometimes parry.

Figures important to the study, contemporary or otherwise, have their years of birth and (if need be) death placed after their names when first mentioned. Writers who enter the discussion more fleetingly are identified with the title of a book. Other figures, whose names are used solely to indicate a cultural movement, are not given dates. The dates of an individual or a title are repeated later, in another chapter, only if they bear on a question being discussed. Whenever a book is cited, the year in brackets after the title indicates its date of original publication, whether in English or another language.

I would like to thank my research assistant, Brooke Cameron, for providing materials and for checking all that I have written. Lou Del Fra, CSC, and Shannon Gayk read the entire typescript, and conversations with them clarified many points. Discussions with

Frank Fisher, Kate Rigby and Regina Schwartz sharpened my thinking at several junctures, and conversations with Cyril O'Regan invariably cast large circles of light on many things. Henry Weinfield read an entire draft and made many valuable comments: I am indebted to him. My wife, Rita Hart, listened to me talk over parts of the book and then read the whole: greater love hath no woman. The Religion and Literature discussion group at the University of Notre Dame generously devoted a seminar to a draft of the final chapter: I have profited from their questions. Jacques Derrida and John Milbank kindly shared their most recent writings with me. Although I wrote this primer without making any quotations, except from the King James Bible, I took pains to make sure that I distorted no one's views, and I would like to thank Romana Huk for helping me locate a remark by Charles Olson and Theresa Sanders for passing on information about the removal of three hundred crosses at Auschwitz in May 1999.

Victoria Roddam invited me to write this primer when I was Visiting Professor of Christian Philosophy at Villanova University in the Fall of 2001. My thanks to her, not least of all for her patience in awaiting the final typescript, and to the Department of Philosophy at Villanova for making my stay so pleasant while I started to think about what I might write. I drafted the book in my second semester at my new intellectual home, the University of Notre Dame. It is a profound pleasure to acknowledge the warm support of my colleagues and students in the Departments of English and Theology. Finally, I am indebted to my new research assistants, Tommy Davis and J.P. Shortall, for their help in checking the proofs.

postmodernism: some guides

To offer oneself as a guide minimally presumes that one knows the locality sufficiently well to be of help to someone unfamiliar with it. An expert can show a novice around modern philosophy or differential calculus or eighteenth-century British literature without worrying all that much about whether it is even possible to perform the task. After all, people more or less agree that there is something called 'modern philosophy', for example, even if they disagree whether it begins with John Locke (1632–1704) or René Descartes (1596–1650), and even if they argue whether it has been done more effectively in recent years in continental Europe or in Britain and the United States. Those very disagreements are the sort of thing to which a thorough and responsible guide would alert us. Yet in presenting oneself as a guide to postmodernism there is reason to doubt whether the task can be done. For people do not agree about what postmodernism is, where to go to see its main sights, or even if one can distinguish its central features from others that are less significant. Several people hailed as central figures in the postmodern landscape reject the label of 'postmodern' in no uncertain terms. Some postmodernists tell us that there is no fixed landscape any more, and after listening to them for long enough we might come to think that their own thoughts and words do not form a stable terrain either. And yet there is no shortage of people offering to take you on a tour.

1

As it happens, here comes a guide. He is wearing a badge with vertical stripes of blue, white and red, and printed over them: *Les tours de postmodernisme*. It seems promising. After all, you've heard that postmodernism is a thoroughly French thing, and so you sign up without delay. The tour will take place in a lecture theater, you are told, and will introduce you to various thinkers and writers. One name has already been written on the board, Jean-François Lyotard (1925–98), and underneath it is the title of one of his books, *The Postmodern Condition: A Report on Knowledge*, originally published in French in 1979. 'It was Lyotard' – the lecturer has begun, speaking in excellent English with only a whiff of a French accent – 'who made a generation attend to the word "postmodern". Of course, the word itself had been used before. It can be found as far back as the 1870s, and perhaps some of you Americans have read Bernard Iddings Bell's book *Postmodernism and Other Essays*? No? Well, it was published in Milwaukee in 1926, and indicated a new kind of religious believer, someone not taken with liberal theology. But as we say in France, *les choses ont changé*, things have changed, and the word now means something else.

'So let us return to Lyotard. The postmodern, he argued, was an attitude of suspicion towards the modern. Why? Because the modern always appeals to a "meta-narrative" of some kind, something that overarches all human activities and serves to guide them: the natural primacy of human consciousness, the fair distribution of wealth in society, and the steady march of moral progress. To be postmodern is to distrust the claim that we can attain enlightenment or peace by the judicious use of reason, that we can become happy or prosperous, that any of our higher goals can be achieved if only we wait and work, work and wait.' He clears his throat. 'If the modern designates the era of emancipation and knowledge, consensus and totalities, then the postmodern marks an attitude of disbelief towards the modern. It is not – I repeat *not* – an epoch that comes after the modern. For Lyotard, the postmodern is what is most radical and irritating in the modern, what offends the canons of good taste: it insists on presenting what we cannot conceptualize, what we cannot find in our experience.

'But I am not a guide to Lyotard,' the lecturer says with a faint smile. 'I work for *Les tours de postmodernisme*, and so I wish to show you the towering figures of postmodernism. To do such a thing would scandalize true postmodernists' (again, he smiles) 'since they mock the monumental. They would think I'm merely pulling a stunt. Then again, a "true postmodernist" is a contradiction in terms, since no postmodernist is entirely comfortable with inherited notions of "truth". No, I'm not tricking you – it's the truth!' And he smiles again, this time for a second longer, before turning around to face the blackboard. Jacques Lacan (1901–81): that is the name he writes on the board, and no sooner has he started to tell you about Lacan – his famous seminars at the Hôpital Sainte-Anne and then at the École Normale Supérieure, his views on Sigmund Freud and what he drew from philosophers from Plato to Martin Heidegger, his extraordinary reading of a story by Edgar Allen Poe, 'The Purloined Letter' – you are puzzled. Is he a psychoanalyst, a philosopher, or an unusual sort of literary critic? Your guide suggests he is all three in one, and your pen is moving quickly as the lecturer scribbles on the board. It seems that Lacan's main concern is the self or what philosophers, reflecting on the theory of subjectivity since Descartes, have called 'the subject', and his theme is how this subject is organized and disorganized by language. We might think that language enriches the self, giving it a greater understanding of the world and its places there, but Lacan sees things quite differently: language impoverishes the subject, strips it of being and meaning.

The guide draws two intersecting circles on the board. One is called 'being' and the other 'meaning'. 'The point of intersection,' he says, 'is the place of the subject: it is the site of two lacks, *being* and *meaning*. Lacan wants us to see the subject as the space of desire.' It turns out, though, that desire is not a raw yearning for any particular object or person in the world. No, it is a longing that has been shaped by metaphor. 'Yes, metaphor,' your guide insists, ' "X *is* Y". And not only metaphor but also metonymy, "X is *contiguous* with Y and takes on some or all of its attributes". You'd like an example? Okay: "a walking stick" is a metonymy (the *stick* is not walking, you are, but with its help), "a boiling kettle" (the *kettle* is not boiling: the water next to the metal is). Get the idea? Good. Now for Lacan the subject stands beside a fragment of what is longed for.' So the subject is motivated by a desire for something not quite symbolic and not quite real: the full-grown man does not want his mother's breast again but unconsciously desires the enjoyment that the maternal breast suggests. 'Of course,' the guide says, smiling ruefully, 'the subject can never be satisfied; we always miss what we aim for, and besides we are always changing and consequently desiring other objects.'

No sooner have you started to grasp how the Lacanian subject turns on those two venerable literary figures, metaphor and metonymy, than your guide is heading elsewhere. Another name is now on the board: Jacques Derrida (1930–). 'He started as a brilliant scholar of phenomenology, the approach to philosophizing devised by Edmund Husserl,' the guide declares, 'and has created a massive body of work, ranging from Plato to Jean-Luc Nancy. As it happens, he wrote a complex and devastating essay on Lacan called "Le facteur de la vérité" (1975) which, like many of Derrida's titles, is impossible to translate: it can mean "the postman of truth" or "the factor of truth", and both are important in the essay.' Derrida has mainly been concerned to show that philosophical concepts are not restricted to philosophical texts: they can be found operating in economics and literature, art criticism and politics, psychoanalysis and theology, pedagogy and architecture. 'He believes that Western thought has always sought firm grounds – Being, God, the Subject, Truth, the Will, even Speech – but that the quest for these grounds can never arrest the play of textual meaning. Those grounds are always figured as moments of presence: God is absolutely pure self-presence, for instance.' The guide pauses and writes a list of texts by Derrida on the board: *Speech and Phenomena, Of Grammatology, Margins of Philosophy, Glas* ... 'One of my favorite essays by him is "Des tours de Babel" (1985). How to translate that? Well, "On Towers of Babel" or equally "Some Towers of Babel" or perhaps "Turns of Babel" or even "Tricks of Babel",' he says, smiling again. 'He reads the old story in Genesis and turns it into an allegory of deconstruction. So he tells us how the Shem tribe wants to make a name for itself by building a tower that will reach all the way to heaven. The Shem want to spread their language over the universe, make everything translatable into their terms. Yahweh, Lord of the Universe, will have none of it, and imposes his own name on the tower, "Babel", and thereby upsets their project. The proper name – Voltaire thought it came from the Babylonian word for "Father" – is heard by the Shem in their language as a common noun, "confusion", and as it happens Yahweh confuses them linguistically: the consequence of their pride is an irruption of different languages. The Shem cannot translate "Babel" because it is a proper name, yet Yahweh requires them to translate it and, in doing so, he creates confusion among them.

'If you like, you could say,' and here the guide pauses for effect, 'that Yahweh *deconstructs* the tower that the Shem want to build. He shows that they cannot render all of reality clearly and without loss into their own language, that the tower is a thoroughly human construction, like all others, and that because it is incomplete and unable

to be completed we can inspect it and see how it has been put together. Derrida condenses much of his teaching into one elegant
French expression, *plus d'une langue*, which without a context to fix
its meaning can signify both "more than one language" and "no more
of one language". There is no higher language to which we can appeal
that will resolve all differences and render everything finally clear to
us. We always have to translate, from one language to another, or within the one language, from one idiom to another. We always translate
and we always have had to: there never has been an original language
or an original text that preceded our endless work of translation.'

So *that's* what deconstruction is, you think, and now you are
smiling with the guide. 'Derrida is an astonishingly good reader' – the
lecturer continues – 'he can show those contemporaries who think
they have abandoned or surpassed philosophy that they maintain a
relation with a ground of some sort, while the commanding philosophers of the past – Plato and Hegel, in particular – offer us opportunities to develop new ways of thinking. The essay he wrote on Lacan
that I mentioned a moment or two ago, "Le facteur de la vérité",
demonstrated that the psychoanalyst was entangled in metaphysics
when he believed himself to be quite free of it.' He looks around and
sees a few puzzled faces, including yours.

' "Metaphysics"? Well, you are right to be puzzled. There are
various definitions of the word, and it's easy to get confused. The
word comes from the Greek *meta ta physica*, meaning what comes
after physics. The word became associated with some highly influential lectures by Aristotle (384–322 BCE), now gathered together
and called the *Metaphysics*; they came after his lectures on nature
called the *Physics*. Long after Aristotle, people thought of the topics
the philosopher considered – things like the nature of being, cause,
unity, numbers – as removed from nature, so metaphysics became
associated with the supersensuous, namely, that which is above or
beyond what our sense experience can register. I can experience this
piece of chalk' (and he dangles a long, white stick before you), 'but I
cannot experience the *essence* of the chalk. Postmodernists tend to
use the word "metaphysics" more generally than do readers of the
Metaphysics. They follow the meaning that the German philosopher
Martin Heidegger (1889–1976) gave to the word. Metaphysics, he
thought, asks the question "What are beings?" but fails to ask the
more fundamental question "What is being?" Because it doesn't ask
that question, it figures being by way of beings, and so we think of
being as a firm ground like God or Mind.'

That said, he moves on. 'Derrida can also show us how to read literary texts more closely and finely than we are used to doing without doing anything like conventional literary criticism. Prose writers like Maurice Blanchot (1907–2003) and James Joyce (1882–1941), and poets like Stéphane Mallarmé (1842–98) and Paul Celan (1920–70), fold philosophical motifs in strange ways in their work and give us opportunities to rethink the concepts we have inherited.'

You are about to ask for an example, but it is already too late. Your guide is now talking about open networks of micropowers, rhizomatics, and the free flow of desire. The names on the board are Gilles Deleuze (1925–95) and Félix Guattari (1930–92), the one a philosopher and the other a writer on anti-psychiatry. They became friends and wrote several books together. Two are especially important, it appears: *Anti-Oedipus* (1983) and *A Thousand Plateaux* (1987). 'Lacan wanted to return to the early Freud, but Deleuze and Guattari set themselves against the preoccupation with the subject that they find in Freud. Desire, they say, does not arise from the subject but is flowing everywhere; in fact, the subject is an effect of desire. There is no original desire for the mother to be satisfied, only a generalized flux of desire that is now formed this way and now that way.' All that is rather a lot to take in, you think to yourself, yet the lecturer is still in full flight. 'The really bold position adopted by Deleuze and Guattari,' he says, 'is the claim that experience is not maintained in the consciousness of a subject. They are radical empiricists, true heirs of the eighteenth-century Scottish philosopher David Hume (1711–76), and they argue that there is no ground of experience, whether in the mind or outside it.' What does all that mean? Luckily, the guide has anticipated your perplexity. 'If Deleuze and Guattari are right,' he says, 'we have to rethink experience and all that goes along with it, especially perception and consciousness, and recognize that the human has no exclusive right to them. That's why *A Thousand Plateaux* discusses desiring machines and genes, evokes "becoming animal" and "the body without organs". The book points us beyond humanism.

'In his own way, Michel Foucault does the same,' he adds, then remembers to write his dates on the board: 1926–84. Now here's a name you've heard before. You've heard that he analyzes the relations between power and knowledge, and now you are taking notes, as best you can, about how his notion of archeology differs from the usual practice of history. 'Where historians attend to continuities and try to set discontinuities within a larger framework of development or evolution, an archeologist like Foucault has no interest in smoothing out the past but prefers to concern himself with rifts, ruptures and contradictions.' The concept 'man' itself is a fairly recent invention, it appears, and if you understand your guide correctly Foucault thinks its time is more or less over. Sovereign man, subject and object of knowledge: he arrived on the scene, according to Foucault, only a few centuries ago, and his demise has been heralded in the narratives of Franz Kafka, Maurice Blanchot and Pierre Klossowski, among others. 'In his later work' – the lecturer continues, and by now your hand is getting tired from taking so many notes – 'Foucault tried to think outside the realm of the subject. He argued that power is everywhere: it is not concentrated in individuals and is not limited to social classes but abides in structures and systems. You can resist power, but you can never get outside it.' The guide is just about to write more names on the board, for there seems to be no end of them, when a bell strikes the hour, and the lecture is over. As you say farewell to your guide you murmur to yourself the names you have already heard, as well as several others you jotted down along the way: *Jean-François Lyotard, Jacques Derrida, Jacques Lacan, Gilles Deleuze, Hélène Cixous, Julia Kristeva ...*

Overhearing you, another guide comes over and says, 'But *that's* not postmodernism, that's just more high culture – worse, élite academic culture. Besides, postmodernism started in the United States and at first had nothing French about it at all. Lyotard merely made postmodernism respectable to professors of English and Philosophy by hitching it to post-structuralism.' He pauses, and you can now take in his badge. It is in American red, white and blue: *Popular PoMo Tours*, it says, and it has a stylish reproduction of the 'Nike' logo underneath. 'The word "postmodern" was coined by American writers and architects in the late 1940s and early 1950s,' he goes on. 'They wanted to signal that they were doing something different, something more risky, than what their modernist moms and dads were doing. But of course it's taken off in all sorts of directions since then, and if you want to find out about it you'd do better to look around Las Vegas than Paris. Here, let me show you the real thing,' he says, 'free of charge. It's my lunch break, after all. Come on, this is my favorite café in the mall.' And before you can say a word he is already on-line. His laptop screens several video-clips of Madonna

('See how she perpetually remakes herself? There *is* no authentic self to be discovered') and some footage from the Gulf War ('What *really* happened in operation "Desert Storm" was the film of it broadcast on CNN'). Then he points out Philip Johnson's AT&T Corporate Headquarters in New York ('See how it cites Roman and Neo-Classical features? See its Chippendale pediment? Johnson makes a pastiche of the architectural past'), an advertisement for Coke ('The *image* is what you really consume'), Mark Tansey's canvas 'Myth of Depth' ('The man walking on the water is Jackson Pollock, and he is calling representation into question, and, with it, presence and, if you think about it, the Christian God as well'), and then runs a sequence from the movie *Blade Runner* (1982), before talking about it in conjunction with the book on which it is based, Philip K. Dick's pulp science fiction novel, *Do Androids Dream of Electric Sheep?* (1968). Hardly a surprise, he lauds an essay by an American, Donna Haraway: 'Manifesto for Cyborgs' (1989). Then he slips into some French names, and keeps going back to two in particular, Jean Baudrillard (1929–) and Roland Barthes (1915–80) ...

'I thought you said that those French scholars don't give a proper sense of postmodernism,' you object. 'You miss the point,' your new guide says. 'Postmodernism takes what it likes from high culture and puts it to work in popular culture. Besides, Barthes and Baudrillard never bought into philosophy as a' – and here his face turns sour – 'master discourse.' 'So you mean that postmodernism is to do with taking things out of their contexts, fragmenting them, focusing on surfaces rather than depths, and, well, *playing* with them?' 'Ah, now you are getting the idea,' says your new guide, and leans back deeply in his chair. 'It's about collage and pastiche, parody and irony. It's the triumph of the visual image over written text,' he says, and slowly strokes his laptop as he speaks. 'And it's the triumph of data and simulation over nature,' he whispers, as though to himself.

You are about to ask him about that when, just behind him, a woman puts down her glass and turns around. Clearly irritated, she says, 'I wouldn't want you to get the wrong impression that postmodernism is only about popular culture. Your friend here' – she looks sharply at him – 'seems to think that only popular culture has benefited from the rejection of overly rigid distinctions between popular and high culture. Some of the really exciting *literature* of our time begins by doing just that, though. The first powerful works of

postmodernism are James Joyce's *Finnegans Wake* (1939) and
Samuel Beckett's *The Unnameable* (1953). Oh, to be sure, they divide
the border separating high art from the everyday, but you can't tell
me that they were written to be part of "obsolescent lit". The postmodern never completely abandoned the modern, and that's a good
thing. Think of Thomas Pynchon's *Gravity's Rainbow* (1973) or Don
DeLillo's *White Noise* (1985). The very books I've been teaching this
morning, as it happens' – she points to Italo Calvino's *If on a Winter's
Night, a Traveler* (1979) and Umberto Eco's *The Name of the Rose*
(1980) on the table before her – 'couldn't have been written without
making reference to high culture. Take Eco's novel,' she says; 'on the
one level it is a quite conventional detective novel while on another
level it is a sophisticated allegory of intertextuality, a reflection on
how all books refer endlessly to other books. That way of combining
the high and the low is called "double coding".'

With her Mont Blanc fountain pen firmly in hand, the woman
who has just been talking is now starting to make what, from the
intensity of her gaze, might well turn out to be a long list of other
postmodern writers you should read – Walter Abish, John Ashbery,
Donald Barthelme, Susan Howe, Alain Robbe-Grillet, Patrick
Süskind ... – when she too is interrupted. Clearly annoyed by what
he has overheard, a young man twists round and says, 'The postmodern isn't something that happens just in Departments of
English or Comp. Lit., although perhaps it would be better were it
confined there.' He trains his aim steadily on the woman, and then
turns to the man still sitting beside you. 'And this fetishism of
popular culture isn't the postmodern, either – you're taking the
effect for the thing itself, if there is just the one thing, which is very
doubtful. What you all need to realize is that postmodernity is a
complex reaction to the terrible failures of modernity. Do I really
need to list them? The Holocaust, the Gulag, the ecological disaster
that's destroying our children's futures even as we speak, and the
sheer destitution of millions of starving people in the third world.'

'The *failures* of modernity!' splutters the defender of literature.
'Hold on a minute. Let me remind you of Jürgen Habermas's essay
"Modernity – An Unfinished Project". It's been around for, like,
twenty years! Besides, as I was just saying, it's a big mistake to think
that the postmodern is a stark rejection of the modern or an advance
over it. And I was about to say that it's another big mistake to think
of people like Einstein and Freud as moderns pure and simple since
they are the ones who unknowingly set in motion the decentered

and groundless world of post-modernity.' But the young man
doesn't have the slightest intention of letting himself be interrupted
for very long. 'Oh yes, I know all that stuff about modernity not
being completed, and that we have a duty still to be enlightened and
rational, brushing our teeth and all that. But I want to tell you something different from what those Frankfurt School people say.' He
takes a testing sip of the steaming *café latte* just set down before him,
then launches into what everyone feels will be a harangue.

'We all know that nation states are far less powerful than before the
Second World War: economics has gone global, and the world econ-
omy is increasingly based on consumption instead of production. We
live in a world of images. At first this brave new world of hyper-reality
and mass media, credit and contingency, seems exciting, though I
assure you it isn't much fun for the poor who live for the most part in
countries burdened with debt accumulated from the first world. And
behind the effervescence there is insecurity and fear. Is it a coincidence
that the most popular sites on the Internet are either pornographic or
religious? It's one thing to strip away the illusions of modernity, quite
another to know how to live without them or, worse, to live with what
they have spawned. With the loss of imperial power, you gain small,
angry states; and with the rise of American internationalism, you gain
international terrorism. What's important about the postmodern is
that it allows us to live without the illusions that modernity dangled
before us – that, if we were reasonable and worked hard, we might all
be free and prosperous and happy. But that doesn't mean we should
spend all our time pondering ads for Nike or reading self-reflexive
novels. We should all be doing something to help those people
excluded by the culture of Coke and Cleverness.' He looks at his watch,
finishes his coffee with one swallow, and nods farewell. He has a lecture
to give. As it happens, all three guides leave together, in florid conversation; and you are left with other names swirling in your mind:
*Homi Bhabha, Zygmunt Bauman, Terry Eagleton, Linda Hutcheon,
Fredric Jameson* ...

'He's far from wrong,' says a young woman sitting behind you,
'although he really should distinguish the postmodern as an historical epoch from the postmodern as an ensemble of styles. And he
should acknowledge that there are some politically engaged postmodernists like Ernesto Laclau and Chantal Mouffe, as well as radical black postmodernists, like Cornel West.' You turn around, and
note that she is wearing an unusual badge:

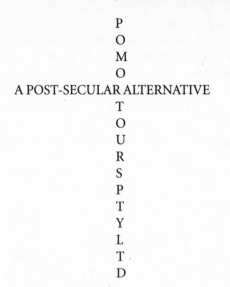

P
O
M
O
A POST-SECULAR ALTERNATIVE
T
O
U
R
S
P
T
Y
L
T
D

'He left just when he was getting to some really interesting issues: the postmodern as a re-enchantment of the world, as a new opportunity for thinking ethics and – I don't know if he would have gotten around to this – a fresh way of approaching the mystery of God.' 'I don't think he was heading in that direction,' you say. 'No, I fear not,' she concedes, 'and I don't think that woman was either: she cited Einstein and Freud but didn't even think to mention Karl Barth, the greatest theologian of the last century, who also argued that we have no foundations in this world and who pointed us beyond humanism. Anyway, let me fill you in on what he wouldn't have said. I've got a full minute before my next tour.' You laugh together, and she leans towards you and starts speaking quickly.

'Modernity was haunted by the *deus absconditus*, the God who withdrew from the world, and put universal reason in his place. But with the end of modernity we glimpse the end of the *hubris* that there can be a universal reason created and cared for by men and women. The postmodern is the site of the post-secular; it's an opportunity for people to develop critiques of modernity and its brash rejection of the divine. Postmodernists are right: there are no fixed essences, only a differential flux. They are mistaken, though, when they think that this implies there can be no values, no meaning, nothing at all, or, worse, that it suggests a world of perpetual assertions and counter-assertions of the will to power. They think in that way because they are in the lingering grip of the modern and its fascination with abstractionism, secularism and nihilism. We can think that flux differently, as a consequence of God creating the world out of nothing. And we can think theology as a discourse that promotes peace simply because, unlike all the secular disciplines, it lays no claim to mastery.'

'Boy, theologians must have changed,' you say, smiling. 'The ones I've heard over the years lay claim to mastery unlimited, and they hardly promote peace! Ever heard of *odium theologicum*, hatred among theologians?' She doesn't rise to the bait, so you change track and go on. 'The guide I hired this morning told me that God performed the first deconstruction when he imposed his name on the Tower of Babel,' you say. 'But before I came this morning I'd heard that Derrida was a nihilist.' 'Sounds like you signed up for *Les tours de postmodernisme*,' she says. 'Say, do their guides still make those awful puns on "tour"?' 'Not that I noticed.' 'Oh good; that's an improvement. But let's go back to your question. Some postmodern Christians think Derrida is a nihilist,' she says, 'although I'm not at all convinced they are right. If you read Derrida well, you can see that he is not attacking the Judeo-Christian God; if anything, he is pointing out that God does not have to be figured as the ground of reality – the first being, the highest being, the being of being – no, God can be God without having to be an unmoved mover or whatever. In fact, Derrida is opening the way to develop a sophisticated non-metaphysical theology, one that offers a sustained rejection of idolatry. It might even enable us to rethink our positive theologies, including the doctrines of the Christ and the Trinity, and make them more genuinely theological.'

'You mean that Derrida is a theologian?' 'No, no: not at all. He's not a believer himself, and his interests are otherwise; but since his critical object is metaphysics, not theology, he looks on with considerable interest to see how deconstruction might work in theology ... Of course, some people think that deconstruction does not direct us to re-elaborate the central doctrines of Christianity but to entrench the death of God. And there are still others who argue that a deconstructive theology is best approached as a quest for justice, that it reveals a general structure of messianicity.' 'Can you explain that last word?' 'Sorry, got to run,' she says. 'My next tour is just about to start. You can come along, if you like.' But you've had quite enough. Somewhat giddy, you write down the names of those she has just mentioned: *John Caputo, Kevin Hart, Jean-Luc Marion, John Milbank, Merold Westphal, Mark C. Taylor, Edith*

Wyschograd ... It's been a long day, and you go home and cannot get to sleep until late.

* * *

'What on earth happened yesterday?' You've woken up, and you have a terrible headache from talking with all those guides. 'What is postmodernism, really?' you ask yourself. 'Did all those guides describe the one phenomenon from different angles, or did they tell me about separate things? And – wait a minute – who on earth are *you*? And how did you get in?' Hi. I'm the author, and you bought my book the other day. So that's how come I'm in your house. Nice place, too. I overheard your questions, and perhaps I can help you, though my answer is bound to be unsatisfactory. Overall, those guides did both: they described postmodernism and described entirely different things. 'How can that be?' It's quite possible because none of your guides took the trouble to draw some fundamental distinctions. I won't promise that once you have those distinctions in place all of postmodernism will become clear to you. It won't. But you will be in a far better position to learn more about it. 'Aren't you biased, though? I remember that one of the guides, right at the end, said that you were one of those people involved with postmodern theology; and I'm not at all sure that I can trust someone who has an axe to grind.'

It's true: I have contributed a little to postmodern theology, but to know where I stand might make it easier for you to judge my remarks. Besides, you are hardly likely to trust a meta-guide to postmodernism, are you, especially after what you were told yesterday? Postmodernists tend to ask *D'où parlez-vous?*, 'Where do you speak from?', and it is a good question. So I should tell you, right at the start, that I'm far from being a wholehearted advocate of postmodernism. I admire Derrida, although you should be aware that he repudiates the label 'postmodernist'. He thinks it marks a historical division between a modern and a postmodern era, and quite rightly he doesn't credit that sort of rupture. And I admire Lévinas and Marion, among others. Are they postmodernists in any important sense of the word? It's debatable. More, though, I enjoy some of those writers who seemed to be in the background of your guide's remarks: Samuel Beckett and Maurice Blanchot, Paul Celan and John Ashbery. Are they postmodern? Well, yes and no. The word

'postmodern' might help bring some of their concerns into focus,
once we begin to understand it, but it surely won't illuminate everything about them. I'll have something to say about that later. Before
then, though, let me distinguish a few elements. You might want to
make yourself some coffee while I talk. And, please, do put some
clothes on.

1. First of all, we need to be aware that the word 'postmodernism' can mean different things in different contexts, and the most
important context is the word to which it refers: 'modernism'. So
what is modernism? Usually, the word signifies a brew of cultural
phenomena that became quite heady in the first twenty or thirty
years of the last century. We can indicate it with some names:
T.S. Eliot and Ezra Pound, James Joyce and Virginia Woolf, Pablo
Picasso and Marcel Duchamp, Henri Matisse and Le Corbusier. In
the Christian religion, though, 'modernism' means something quite
different. Theological modernism also started to gain energy around
the turn of the twentieth century. Its proponents – Friedrich von
Hügel, Alfred Loisy and George Tyrell, among others – ran several
lines: that religion is at heart a matter of experience, even feeling;
that religious impulses are ultimately unconscious and reason is
alien to them; that doctrine is at best a symbolic representation of
spiritual needs, at worst a dead hand on religious life, and that it
changes over time. Both modernisms can be seen as movements in a
larger historical epoch called modernity that started in the
seventeenth century, if you trust the philosophical time line, or the
sixteenth century, if you prefer the literary time line. From now on,
'modernism' will denote cultural modernism, and I will specifically
talk of 'theological modernism' if I need to do so. In fact, though,
I won't be doing that for some time, let alone talking about
'theological postmodernism'. We've got quite enough on our
plate for the moment, don't you think?

2. Now we have to draw a line, if we can, between postmodernism and postmodernity. Let's begin with a placing shot: *postmodernism* is an open set of approaches, attitudes and styles to art and
culture that started by questioning or exceeding or fooling with one
or more aspects of modernism. The blurry group of ideas we call
postmodernism started to come into focus in the 1950s and 60s in
America. Irving Howe talked, rather disparagingly, of postmodernist writers in 1959. Unlike the modernists, they had no critical
edge, he thought. Leslie Fiedler gave a talk at Rutgers University in
June 1965 which he entitled 'The New Mutants', and in that lecture

he evoked something he dubbed 'post-Modernist literature', and spoke of it with more enthusiasm than Howe had done. Fiedler had in mind authors such as John Barth, Anthony Burgess, William Burroughs, William Golding, Harry Matthews and Kurt Vonnegut, Jr. Anyone who had read Barth's *The Sot-Weed Factor* (1960) would have realized that the author was poking fun at realistic narrative, while admirers of Burroughs's *The Naked Lunch* (1959) would have picked up that he was using collage in preference to linear narration. The word 'postmodern' had been used even before Howe and Fiedler, though. They could have quoted Randall Jarrell's review of Robert Lowell's *Lord Weary's Castle*. That collection of poems appeared in 1946, and it was around that time that some architects started to use the word. Later, it was much used when talking about ideas and buildings by Philip Johnson and Michael Graves, James Stirling and Robert Venturi. Nowadays it's not much used in architecture, despite the efforts of Peter Eisenman. Most people today would think of Lowell's early poetry as late modernist instead of postmodernist, and admirers of postmodern poetry would point to John Ashbery or Emmanuel Hocquard or Lyn Hejinian as favored exemplars. In these writers one finds an attention to surfaces rather than depths, an affirmation of the everyday rather than a commitment to high seriousness, discontinuities rather than unities, and a thoroughly decentered subjectivity.

Pastiche and irony, collage and non-functional form: all these were beginning to color American artistic counter-cultures in the late 1950s and the 1960s. As the sixties gave way to the seventies those different threads started to be tied together by literary critics working in the United States – Ihab Hassan and William V. Spanos are two prominent names – and before long they found their way to France. There Lyotard, Baudrillard and others retied them, adding some local threads, and only a little while later the value-added product was imported by American colleges and universities and then exported from America and France all over the English-speaking world. There were three main local threads used by the French. The first was a rejection of foundations or origins that are held to be given naturally, inevitably or universally. The second was a rejection of realism, namely, the thesis that language, when used properly, can tell us the truth about reality. And the third was a rejection of humanism: man, considered as the subject and object of knowledge, is no longer held to be sovereign but is regarded as an effect of desires or discourses or power systems.

And so postmodernism was spread across the globe. Having left America as experimental art, it came back as high theory; and teachers and students in a thousand cities started to read that same experimental art through the newly ground lenses of theory.

Now *postmodernity* is commonly taken to denote the historical period in which we live today, what is taken to have succeeded the modern age. Historians with a taste for periodization will sometimes say that the postmodern era started after the Second World War, although you can always find indications of change before then. In the same way, no sooner does someone say that postmodern literature started to emerge in the 1950s than another person will find a literary work from the past that has some, if not all, of the same features: Laurence Sterne's *Tristram Shandy* (1759–65) and Jonathan Swift's *A Tale of a Tub* (1704) are cases in point. That's the sort of thing Lyotard has in mind when he insists that the postmodern is an attitude, not an age. Yet even if one is dubious about dividing history into periods, each with one or more guiding spirits, one will surely recognize that the world has changed in a distinctive way over the last half century. By the mid-1950s most American homes had at least one television set: the Cold War was characterized by the domestic entrenchment of visual culture, and by 1989, when the Berlin Wall was dismantled, baby boomers had become at ease with personal computers. Ten years later they were comfortable with the Internet. That same generation has slowly learned that the nation state, to which so many hopes of the modern era were attached, cannot provide the security that it promised to provide. It is perhaps the only thing in the last few decades that has been slow, for postmodern times are characterized by speed. We live in perpetual acceleration.

And yet society has stalled. There is appalling poverty in the United States: in Chicago and Los Angeles, New York and Washington, DC many children cannot find enough to eat. With the end of post-war prosperity in Europe, America and Australia, the financial market has been deregulated, and those economies that depend on commodities have suffered badly in recent years. There are international companies – Exxon, General Motors and Shell, to name just three – with more buying power than the smaller economies of Europe, Africa and the Pacific Rim; and to whom, if anyone, are the International Monetary Fund, the World Bank and the World Trade Organization ultimately responsible? We have come to live in a world where religious fanaticism has not been quietly sidelined by rational enlightenment, as was once hoped, but has come to speak loudly from competing political sites. Somehow it has happened that we talk of 'clean war' and use images of the death of innocents as 'infotainment'. That same world is threatened by rogue states with nuclear capacity, not to mention bio- and cyber-terrorists. It is shocked by the spread of AIDS and not shocked enough by ecological breakdown: the great forests, the planet's lungs, get smaller and smaller each year. Osama bin Laden's attack on the World Trade Center and the Pentagon on September 11, 2001 has made the entire first world insecure: he did not attack buildings, plain and simple, he targeted symbols. International capitalism and postmodern culture have been in partnership for decades. Yet clearly not all the world enjoys seeing the happy couple parading around the world as if they owned it.

Apocalyptic narratives are a familiar part of postmodernity, and some of them, like Y2K, just fizzle out. All these narratives form the background for revivals of the gothic, the gnostic and the pagan. To flick from channel to channel on daytime TV is to encounter angels and vampires, aliens and cyborgs, to be assured of the imminence of the end times by preachers and to have Nostrodamus's predictions seriously discussed by apparently well-educated guests on talk shows. Postmodernity can be construed as what occurred to the world when we stopped trusting in modernity, when order and reason, moral progress and enlightenment, ceased to be high values we held in common. Modernity, we realized, may have filled us with illusions about what humans could achieve, but it also shielded us from many religious and political horrors. Hitler and Stalin appear as egregious exceptions to a plausible world order only if one has a confirmed trust in the power of human beings everywhere to become more democratic, more rational, and more humane. Yet if postmodernity declares 'less of modernity' it also affirms 'more of modernity'. The postmodern age can give us everything modernity offered, it is said, but without its abstractions, its unreachable social ideals and its moralizing. For the postmodernist, there is no one 'modernity'. So we should not say 'more of modernity' but 'more of modernit*ies*'. We can take the bold advances in medical science and digital technology, we can embrace the emancipation of women and Martin Luther King, Jr.'s dream, and we can keep the constitutions and bills of rights drawn up in the eighteenth century. And we can leave behind everything that seems implausible or utopian, begin-ning with the welfare state. I dare say the poor will be abandoned before very long: modernity had a place for the poor – the future, where all would be well – but postmodernity has no such place for them. If postmodernism attracts many political liberals, post-modernity chimes nicely with the interests of political conservatives.

3. We also need to distinguish postmodernism from post-structuralism. I've already said a few things about that: we've seen that American postmodernism was taken up by the French, reworked in a philosophical vein, and exported back to the United States. The first guide you had the other day, the smooth fellow from *Les tours de postmodernisme*, spent almost all his time talking about post-structuralists, not postmodernists. To be fair, the two 'isms' have come to penetrate one another, but there are important differ-ences between them nonetheless. The first thing to note is obvious: post-structuralism contains a reference to structuralism, the domin-ant intellectual discourse in France in the 1950s and early 1960s. Claude Lévi-Strauss (1908–) is the father figure of the movement, especially in the social sciences, although he drew very deeply from the structural linguistics of Ferdinand de Saussure (1857–1913) and Roman Jakobson (1896–1982) who inspired other structuralists such as A.J. Greimas (1917–92) and Gérard Genette (1930–). It was Saussure who distinguished *langue*, the system of language, from *parole*, the spoken word. The former is social; the latter, individual. And it was Saussure who taught us to separate the diachronic aspect of language, its passage through history, from the synchronic aspect, its invariant structures at any given moment.

No speaker is conscious of those structures while uttering sentences, and in the same way, Lévi-Strauss thought, other social institutions are governed by rules of which no individual member is conscious. He was especially interested in myths. Only when we become aware of the social structures of myths, he argued, can we make sense of them; and those structures appear only when we relate all the myths of a given society to one another. All the thinkers now called post-structuralists – principally, Jacques Derrida, Michel Foucault and Jacques Lacan – maintained a rapport with structural-ism, even when they became critical of it and even though their intellectual context may have included ideas and schools foreign to structuralism. Derrida, for instance, emerged as a student of phe-nomenology; and he attracted attention in his first writings not only by finding a doctrine of signs in Husserl's writings (and submitting it to a stringent deconstruction) but also by exposing and undoing a metaphysics at work in structuralism.

All three of the main post-structuralists are French, yet the label itself is American, and I can tell you a story about how this came to be. In October 1966 a conference was convened at the Johns Hopkins University in Baltimore. Its title: 'Critical Languages and the Science of Man'. Its brief: to introduce structuralism to the United States. Eminent representatives of the new movement spoke at the conference, including Roland Barthes and Jacques Lacan, and on the last day the young Derrida presented a paper, 'Structure, Sign and Play in the Discourse of the Human Sciences'. Among other things, Derrida developed there a close reading of Lévi-Strauss that convicted him of a nostalgia for innocence that recalled Jean-Jacques Rousseau (1712–78). Structuralism did not last a week in the United States; almost immediately it was overtaken by post-structuralism!

Of course, that's not the whole story. As early as 1956 Paul de Man, who participated in the conference at Johns Hopkins and who became well known as a post-structuralist himself, had argued that formalism was a dead end. And in America Derrida was widely taken to be a structuralist for five or six years after the conference. That said, the word 'post-structuralism' was coined in the United States, started to circulate there in the mid–late 1960s, and was used to describe diverse intellectual currents in Europe. Sometimes the word is used simply to denote those thinkers who came after the structuralists. For example, it has been applied to the philosopher Emmanuel Lévinas (1906–95) who developed a highly original ethics by refiguring phenomenology and who never showed the slightest interest in structuralism. Over the decade of the seventies especially, feminists and Marxists tried to rethink their positions by way of post-structuralism and, in the process, inflected it in various ways.

It must be said that the French themselves have been more con-cerned with writers who, to Americans, are modernists or late modernists rather than postmodernists. Stéphane Mallarmé and Franz Kafka, Raymond Roussel and Lautréamont: these are the names one encounters in the writings of the French post-structuralists, and they are prized there for having the potential to transgress aesthetic and social norms. How ironic then that when post-structuralism started to be influential in the United States it came declaring itself to be transgressive but armed with – of all things! – a canon of *modernists*. It is also ironic that one had to do a lot of homework before one could be transgressive in the desired French manner. British and American students and teachers were often unprepared for the range and depth of philosophical reference in the new thought. For the French not only begin studying philosophy in the final year of secondary school, the *classe de philosophie*, but also have a quite different canon of philosophical texts than is taught in the English-speaking world. Many years of reading the 'master thinkers' – Hegel and Nietzsche, Husserl and Heidegger – were required before English-speaking admirers of post-structuralism could even contemplate stepping out of line! Looking back a decade, American postmodern prose and poetry seemed so much more experimental and so much more fun than the texts of philosophy and psychoanalysis that replaced them. In the 1970s and early 1980s, however, it became *de rigueur* to read those works with reference to French thinkers who had been yoked together in a violent manner by advocates of this strange new thing, post-structuralism.

4. Two other words are sometimes used in connection with post-modernism, and it's a good idea to be familiar with them. The first is *post-humanist*. We've already touched on it. All the guides you talked with the other day stressed that postmodernism is highly skeptical about the subject. For European thinkers philosophical modernity started with Descartes and his emphasis upon consciousness as foundational for our knowledge of the world. *Cogito ergo sum*, he declared, 'I think, therefore I am.' And this focus on a coherent, unified subject has been an abiding concern of many philosophers since Descartes, most notably Immanuel Kant (1724–1804) and Edmund Husserl (1859–1938). It has been said that postmodern thinkers have erased the subject, but no such thing has happened. At most the subject has been resituated with respect to discourse or desire or power. One of the burdens of Blanchot's critical writing has been the loss of the power to say 'I'. On his understanding, there is something older than the *cogito*: not an act of thought at all but a ceaseless murmur of language without a magnetizing center of con-sciousness. In quite different ways Derrida and Foucault have been influenced by this idea. For Derrida, the 'I' is never fully self-present; it always presupposes a relation with its own general absence, namely death. And for Foucault, the priority of the philosophical 'I think' is contested by the 'I speak'. Speech and writing, Foucault maintains, will disperse the 'I' sooner than bring it to a sharp focus.

Technology, not philosophy, is what excites some advocates of post-humanism. There is nothing inevitable about the current biological form of the human being, they argue; it has been different in the past, and we can expect it to change in the future. We can guide and accelerate that change with the help of bio-technology: chemical supplements in our diet can increase intelligence and memory, artificially created bacteria can be released into the intestines to fight infections, new tissue can be implanted in the brain and micro-chips can be inserted into bodily organs to encourage regeneration. The cyborg need not be a science-fiction fantasy; within a generation or two it is likely to become the norm, at least among the powerful and the wealthy. Post-humanism is clearly an extension of two of modernity's strongest wishes: to arrest temporal flux and to preserve the self. And if the new bio-technologies plainly wish to preserve the 'I' rather than disperse it, that does not bar them from being postmodern; it merely shows that post-modernity accepts contradictions. Besides, if one remembers and thinks, lives and breathes because of micro chips and gene therapy, can one say without qualification that one has remained an unadulterated 'I'?

5. The second word you will sometimes hear in conversations about the postmodern is *post-metaphysical*. We live in a post-metaphysical age, people say, although when questioned they are seldom clear about what that means, if it means anything at all. Seeds of the idea can be traced back to Kant who, in his *Critique of Pure Reason* (1781; second edition, 1787), sought to limit the scope of metaphysics in order to make room for faith. In the first half of the twentieth century some British and American philosophers went beyond Kant, and certainly beyond his religious impetus for criticizing metaphysics, and attempted to bypass or reject metaphysics in part or whole. If philosophy is refigured as a rigorous study of language, we can stop being bothered by pseudo-problems, they thought. Yet it is Martin Heidegger (1889–1976) to whom postmodernists usually turn when evoking the idea of the post-metaphysical. Beginning with his lectures on Friedrich Nietzsche (1844–1900) delivered at Freiburg in the late 1930s, Heidegger spoke of the end of Western metaphysics. From the ancient Greeks to Nietzsche himself, Heidegger maintained, philosophers have been guided by the wrong question. They have asked 'What are beings?' rather than 'What is being?' and accordingly they have mistakenly regarded being by way of beings.

To grasp being, the tradition says, we must determine beings as a whole and/or as the highest being. In doing that, Heidegger thinks, metaphysics has constituted itself as onto-theology. Let's take a moment to get clear about this word. The first and last parts are easy: 'onto' comes from the Greek *to on*, 'that which is', and *logos* means 'laying out', 'study' or 'word'. It's the middle part that is more difficult, and Heidegger did not help when he wrote the word as 'onto-theology' rather than 'onto-theiology'. Theology is the study of God, *theos*, but theiology is the study of the highest being, *theion*. Onto-theiology is therefore the study of the unity of beings and the highest being. What unifies beings? Well, the highest being. If you think of God as the highest being then onto-theiology becomes onto-theology. But neither Heidegger nor many theologians think in that way. You can't pray to something that happens to be the highest being, different only in species from every other being, Heidegger said. God must transcend the order of beings. So it is best to talk of onto-theiology. Philosophers have disagreed about what is the highest being or the highest ground. You might say it is the Platonic forms, or human consciousness, or the will, or something else. Heidegger talks of how these things have been thought by way of presence, and Derrida coined the expression 'the metaphysics of presence'. Derrida accords 'presence' a vast scope: it is an object's temporal status, a subject's presence to itself or another subject, and the determination of being as presence. Our deepest, most intractable, presupposition is that being – whether it be understood as God, consciousness, substance, truth or the will – is enduring presence; and that presupposition cannot be dislodged until we finally get over metaphysics. That is no easy task, not least of all because the modern form of the metaphysics of presence is technology. For Heidegger, the post-humanists who celebrate the genetic engineering of the human would be a group of shameless and hardened metaphysicians.

Only if we step back into the ground of metaphysics, Heidegger maintained, can we understand metaphysics properly; and that step requires us to respond to the call of being. That gesture is dubious, Lévinas complains: Heidegger rejects the objectifying presence of technology while nonetheless affirming *Anwesen*, the coming-into-presence of being. And Derrida objects that we can mark the *closure* of metaphysics, though never reach its *end*. Those people who think they have freed themselves from metaphysics can always be shown to have entrenched it all the more thoroughly. We are 'post-metaphysical', if we are, solely in the sense that we have become more aware of the ways in which covert appeals to presence structure our world.

6. Finally, it would be helpful to know a little more about what separates postmodernism and the *avant garde*. I said earlier that

American postmodern writing styled itself as *avant garde*, and it could be argued that it was one of the final manifestations of that phenomenon. The idea of art being *avant garde*, ahead of its time, goes back to the visual arts in nineteenth-century France, and Édouard Manet's paintings have as good a claim as any to mark the birth of the notion. 'Le déjeuner sur l'herbe' (1863), for example, does not stop at rejecting academic conventions in art but, in placing figures in contemporary costume (and one quite naked) in a pastoral setting, plainly wishes to outrage bourgeois taste. It is the artistic movements of the first decades of the twentieth century – cubism, futurism, surrealism and vorticism – that we associate most strongly with the *avant garde*. The sheer proliferation of those irruptive 'isms' in Europe after the First World War testifies to one aspect of the *avant garde*: it is short-lived. All these emanations of modernism sought to contest what counted as art at the time, and each contestation exposed new possibilities while destroying itself in the process. Yet modernism was more than just a temporary home for the *avant garde*. A fundamentally optimistic movement, it was always committed in advance to a future better than the present; and since the demise of modernism, all *avant garde* movements have retained a link with it. The New York School of painters and poets remains the best candidate to be considered as both *avant garde* and postmodern, and yet the work of that movement would go out of focus were we to detach all reference to modernism. One can certainly find traits of the postmodern in the poetry of John Ashbery – an interest in surfaces rather than depths, a disposition to debunk, to let form call the shots with respect to content, and so forth – yet his poetry retains essential links with cubism. 'Soonest Mended', 'Self-Portrait in a Convex Mirror' and 'A Wave' all seek to present experience from different perspectives at the one time.

The very idea of the *avant garde* implies a linear view of artistic history, a view that is inconsistent with postmodernist assumptions about the world. No wonder then that, in order to maintain the idea, a number of postmodernists have come to talk of being the 'post *avant garde*' or the 'trans *avant garde*'. To be *avant garde* one must reject convention, but what if it has become conventional to reject convention? To be *avant garde* one must adopt a marginal position with regard to the art world, but what if the art world actively seeks to consecrate the marginal? The questions can be multiplied, but one does not need to do so in order to recognize that the idea of the *avant garde* may have reached its limit with postmodernism. In the 1970s and early 1980s it seemed for a short while as though the adjective '*avant garde*' was more appropriate to literary critics, philosophers and psychoanalysts than to artists. Post-structuralism was promoted as exceeding convention, affirming the marginal, and exposing us to a new and perhaps monstrous future. Like all manifestations of the *avant garde*, though, it was utopic and could last only a short time.

* * *

Jorge Luis Borges has a beguiling tale 'Of Exactitude in Science' in his collection *A Universal History of Infamy* (1973) in which the cartographers of an empire become so adept at their craft that they devise a map in one-to-one correspondence with the land itself. With the decline of the empire, the map is no longer honored; it falls into disrepair. Years later, travelers encounter scraps of it blown around by the desert winds. In his essay 'Simulacra and Simulations' (1981), Jean Baudrillard suggests that the tale cannot be told of postmodernity, for now we have lost the priority of the terrain with respect to the map. For us, he muses, perhaps the map comes before the territory; and were explorers to encounter the postmodern empire they would find scraps of reality being blown this way and that. Yet there is more truth to be learned about our situation, he suggests, by recognizing that there is no longer any substantial difference between reality and map. Unlike the moderns, unlike the Shem, we do not believe it is even possible to render all of reality intelligible to ourselves. We no longer live with the real but with the hyper-real: signs have replaced referents.

If Baudrillard is correct, none of the guides to postmodernism that you encountered the other day can give you a proper tour of the territory. For the postmodern offers them no way of distinguishing terrain and map. Yet each of them managed to show you something, even if they ended up pointing out different things, and that should give you pause. Are the central features of the postmodern the works of Derrida, Foucault and Lacan? Or are they the writings of John Barth and William Burroughs? Or, again, are they images of Coke and Nike? When we are looking for the postmodern are we right to search for the secular and the nihilistic? Or should we be attending to manifestations of the post-secular?

I have tried to distinguish postmodernism and postmodernity, and if one looks from sufficiently far away there is a clear line between the two. After all, there are many people alive today who dislike postmodern art and who reject postmodern assumptions about culture and society. Yet, like it or not, they are living in a world of mass media, virtual money and hyper-real advertising. The more closely one inspects the border between postmodernism and postmodernity the more gaps will appear. Ordinary people who never read French philosophy or difficult American fiction consume images at home, at the mall, and on the way to both places; and those images strongly influence how they dispose of their virtual money. Yet no line of credit is endless, and hyper-reality has consequences that end in what seem to the poor and the hungry to be all too real.

further reading

Baudrillard, Jean. 'Simulacra and Simulations', in his *Selected Writings*, ed. and introd. Mark Poster. Stanford: Stanford University Press, 1988, 166–84.

Bové, Paul A., ed. *Early Postmodernism: Foundational Essays.* Durham: Duke University Press, 1995.

Derrida, Jacques. 'Deconstruction and the Other', in *Dialogues with Contemporary Continental Thinkers: The Phenomenological Heritage*, by Richard Kearney. Manchester: Manchester University Press, 1984, 107–26.

Foster, Hal, ed. *Anti-Aesthetic: Essays on Postmodern Culture.* Port Townsend: Bay Press, 1983.

Lyotard, Jean-François. *The Postmodern Condition: A Report on Knowledge*, trans. Geoff Bennington and Brian Massumi, foreword Frederic Jameson. Minneapolis: The University of Minnesota Press, 1984.

——. *The Postmodern Explained to Children: Correspondence 1982–1985*, trans., ed. Julian Pefanis and Morgan Thomas. Sydney: Power Publications, 1992.

Venturi, Robert, Denise Scott Brown and Steven Izenour. *Learning from Las Vegas: The Forgotten Symbolism of Architectural Form.* Cambridge: MIT Press, 1972.

chapter two

the loss of origin

We saw in the first chapter that there is no single viewpoint that can unify postmodernism. Perhaps there are no two or three ideas that can do so, either. And perhaps it is simply impossible to reduce postmodernism to a knot of philosophical theses in the first place. It might well be that postmodernists work with particular attitudes and styles – incredulity and irony, for example – that cannot be dissociated from what they do. Nonetheless I would like to dig beneath the surface of postmodernism and retrieve bits and pieces of three theories that I believe are widely, if sometimes covertly, held among its advocates and practitioners.

Not long after you have started to talk with a postmodernist, especially if it is someone influenced by post-structuralism, you will find that person arguing for *anti-essentialism*. There are various forms of it, depending on what 'essentialism' is taken to mean. One of the most widespread forms amounts to the contention that there is no natural or universal essence to being human: everything to do with our state has been historically formed and culturally conditioned. The position has appealed to liberals, especially feminists and socialists, as well as to post-humanists. For if being human has been determined in history it can also be changed in history, whether in the interest of forming a more just society or in the desire to transform the human to the next stage of our existence. Some anti-essentialists chew over the old question 'What is it to be human?' and either criticize humanist answers to it or try to give better answers themselves. Others think it gets us nowhere and

should be replaced by other questions such as 'How can we understand our finitude?' or 'How can we act to prevent another
Auschwitz from occurring?' Slightly less familiar because more
technical is the anti-essentialist line that there are no meanings that
are independent of the mind to which we can appeal in order to fix
the sense of the sentences we utter. Of course, no philosophers today
actually hold that there are meanings floating outside the mind.
Meaning is intentional, they agree; it is always rooted in
consciousness, even if it also has a social dimension. What anti-
essentialists object to are the simpler positions in the theory of
meaning. There is the referential theory of meaning, in which the
proper name ('George Bush') is the basic unit of meaning; and there
is the ideational theory of meaning, in which concepts precede
linguistic expression. Without a referent to which it is clearly bound,
a word can change its sense over the years. And not only words but
also concepts: they too have lives of their own.

To adopt a version of anti-essentialism will strongly influence
how you approach any of the arts. Postmodern theorists tell us that
essentialists who read a novel by Emily Brontë or look at a portrait
by Sir Joshua Reynolds will forever be seeking to pull out deep truths
about the human condition. All this is sometimes said in a slightly
superior manner, and the people being patronized usually object to
being called essentialists in the first place. With regard to philosophers the accusation is usually very wide of the mark: no philosopher today of any repute holds either the simple referential theory of
meaning or the ideational theory of meaning. These people might
agree, though, that they are humanists of one stripe or another. The
theorists will also point out that essentialists or humanists usually
attempt to unify the work by way of interpretation. Read the same
work through anti-essentialist lenses, they suggest, and you will not
be hampered by focusing on truths that can be universalized or by
trying to see the whole text in a single sustained vision. It is more
likely that you will seek to put what you learn about characters and
their situations to use in ethics or politics. 'Read Charles Dickens to
understand the sufferings of the poor', it might be said, 'and read
Robert Antelme to imagine the conditions under which you might
treat men and women as sub-human.' As an anti-essentialist, you
will not be tempted to bypass, overlook or reduce those episodes or
descriptions that run counter to an overall interpretation. In fact,
those things might suggest rival interpretations of the work that do
not cohere and do not go away. All this comes by way of postmodern

literary criticism. It needs to be pointed out, however, that some of
the insights we associate with postmodernism were put to work long
before it was refined in universities as 'theory'. Artistic innovation
can and often does anticipate philosophical theorizing. You have
only to read Raymond Roussel's *Impressions d'Afrique* (1910) or
Michel Leiris's meditation on 'Persephone' in *Biffures* (1948) to see
how to write without being regulated by referents or concepts that
are held to precede language.

You are also likely to find postmodernists urging you to accept a
form of *anti-realism*. Again, the position can be formulated in
various ways, depending on what the person understands by
'realism'. Metaphysical anti-realism is twinned with metaphysical
realism, for instance, while truth anti-realism is the debating partner
of truth realism. Some philosophers of science are realists: they
think that scientists can discover facts about nature that are quite
independent of the process of investigation. Others are anti-realists.
They posit that theoretical entities – items that we cannot observe,
like electrons and genes – are no more than convenient fictions.
Science for them is not in the business of discovering facts about
nature but of constructing schemas and concepts that help us to
predict what will happen. You will also find anti-realists in the field
of ethics, and as you would expect they frame the doctrine with their
own concerns in mind. They deem that there are no normative rules
about what we ought or ought not to do in a given situation, or, if
you like, that there are no normative rules about what is reasonable
or unreasonable to do in that situation. It needs to be said that,
without contradicting yourself, you can be a realist in one area of
philosophy and an anti-realist in another. So you might be a realist
in the philosophy of science and an anti-realist in the philosophy of
mathematics. Many postmodernists hold forms of both metaphysical and truth anti-realism: there is no reality that is independent of the mind, and no truth that enjoys that status either. Usually,
they will deny that there is a correspondence between language and
reality. People who take this stand urge us to accept that language
does not simply transmit information but partly constructs what it
communicates. We cannot have objective knowledge of reality
because we cannot step outside language. Anti-realism with regard
to truth leads different people to do different things: philosophers
will become pragmatists or cultural relativists, while novelists will
write stories in which language does not mirror reality. Don DeLillo
in *White Noise* (1985) and Peter Carey in *Oscar and Lucinda* (1988),

for instance, tell their stories through the voices of unreliable narrators.

Finally, sooner or later you are sure to encounter a postmodernist who argues for *anti-foundationalism*, the claim that our knowledge of the world rests on no secure ground. Western philosophy from Socrates to C.I. Lewis, you will be told, has been the history of attempts to secure a firm foundation for knowledge; and it is likely that, of the modern philosophers, Descartes and Leibniz will be cited first. Descartes sought to doubt everything until he came upon indubitable bedrock, which he did when he realized that he could not doubt that he was thinking. Hence the bold utterance you heard yesterday: *cogito ergo sum*, I think, therefore I am. In the same spirit but oriented to different problems, Gottfried Leibniz (1646–1716) formulated the principle of sufficient reason: nothing happens unless there is a cause or a determining reason. Anti-foundationalism is usually formulated as an epistemological position: it concerns the status of our claims to knowledge. In modern European philosophy, however, it sometimes slides imperceptibly into an ontological position: the status of our being in the world is raised.

It is not hard to see how this occurs, for we tend to think of reality as supporting us in some way. There must be some ground beneath our feet, we tell ourselves. At the same time, when a *fons et origo*, a foundation and origin, is offered to people it is not uncommon for them to want to know what supports *that* ground. We have all come across people, even adults, who do not accept that God is the ultimate origin because they want to know how God came into being. To take the question at all seriously is to countenance an infinite regress: the God who created the heavens and the earth was created by a greater God who, in turn, was created by a yet greater God who ... – you get the idea. I am reminded of the story, probably apocryphal, about the old woman living in an isolated part of the far south of the United States who believed that the earth is carried on the back of a giant turtle. When asked by some smart city boy what supports the turtle, she is reported to have replied, 'It's turtles all the way down!'

Each of these three theories – anti-essentialism, anti-realism and anti-foundationalism – can be formulated in stronger or weaker versions. It all depends on what one is opposing. Some contemporary foundationalists, for instance, do not accept that we can ever find an irreformable ground for our knowledge, as Descartes believed he had discovered. They content themselves with a more relaxed account: perceptual experience, they think, provides us with beliefs that are as basic as we are ever likely to get. Especially once you step outside Departments of Philosophy, it is common for post-modernists to conceive essentialism, realism and foundationalism solely in their more naive versions; and, not unreasonably, this sometimes brings the charge that they are caricaturing philosophy. 'No one has held a simple referential theory of meaning since Frege published "On Sense and Reference" in 1892! If you want to refute a referential account of meaning, at least consider one of the sophisti-cated theories that people actually hold!' 'I've never even *met* a Cartesian foundationalist, and here are postmodernists telling me that *all* philosophers are committed to that sort of foundationalism!' Such are the sort of exasperated remarks that irritated analytic philosophers make when encountering one of the less rigorous strains of postmodernism. Of course, not all postmodernists are anti-essentialist, anti-realist and anti-foundationalist. Luce Irigaray (1930–), especially in her work on sexual difference, has been an important voice in postmodern feminism, yet in the 1980s she was repeatedly criticized for biological and psychic essentialism. By the same token, a good many people are anti-essentialists or anti-realists or anti-foundationalists but are not postmodernists. They have never read the novels of Alain Robbe-Grillet or discussed Charles Moore's 'Piazza d'Italia' (1978) in New Orleans; they would never dream of buying a book by Jean-François Lyotard or Jean Baudrillard; they do not care for the music of John Cage or for the paintings of Jackson Pollock, Willem De Kooning or any other members of the New York School; and wandering down the strip at Las Vegas has no appeal to them at all.

Postmodernists differ from these people because, among other things, they hold other attitudes to culture, act out other styles, and have other interests. They like living in and through a virtual world where you can assume different genders on the Internet, or they think that Frank O'Hara's poems are fun, or they find that parody and pastiche in 'The Simpsons' is cool. Also, more often than not, they differ from them because they affirm versions of the three theories we've been considering that loosely imply each other. With some people the understanding can be detailed and precise. And with others it can be a bit vague: 'There are no abiding essences in human beings,' they say, 'and *therefore* no normative rules and *there-fore* also nothing that could plausibly constitute a set of basic beliefs.'

Much close reasoning would be needed to justify each 'therefore'. Notice that all three theories are framed negatively: essentialism, realism and foundationalism are *rejected*. If this appeals to a certain iconoclasm in some postmodernists (regardless of a fascination they might have otherwise with images), it also gives them commitments that are quite modest, sometimes far too modest to get much done as philosophical theories. That said, the three negative positions imply convictions that can be, and usually are, held affirmatively. If the negative aspect of postmodernism is characterized by irony and incredulity, its positive aspect can surprise one with its openness, its generosity, and its general lack of stuffiness. These are the things that often attract people to postmodernism in the first place: a celebration of difference, a taste for alterity and excess, an endorsement of plurality and play, and a feel for surfaces.

I want to introduce postmodernism by way of anti-foundationalism. I think that is the best approach to take, partly because you hear more postmodernists talk against firm grounds than speak against essences or objective reality. Partly, too, I want to adopt that approach because it raises some interesting questions about what counts as postmodern and what does not. People affirm anti-foundationalism for all sorts of reasons. It can be used to attack humanism. The human, it is argued, has no permanent base in reason, consciousness or even biology. And it can be used to reform humanism: you do not need a perspective-free site in order to justify the view that men and women can solve their problems without appealing to anything outside themselves. Anti-foundationalism can bolster the case against belief in the Judeo-Christian God ('God is dead!') and it can be used to explain how belief in Jesus Christ is justified ('Christian faith lives in and through the words of the New Testament, and does not need to base itself on secular reason'). If you take a step away from contemporary debates, you can see that skepticism with regard to unshakable grounds is not a new item on the agenda of Western thought; it has been around since the ancient Greeks. Today, it has come to enjoy far more support among philosophers of all camps than foundationalism – well, at least classical foundationalism – can muster. And yet it still excites sharp responses from its detractors. Speak against final grounds, they say, and you will undermine the very possibility of establishing knowledge claims, truth, civic values and morally decent courses of action. Not only that, anti-foundationalism also compromises its own intelligibility. For it offers itself as a general truth that applies to all other theories while denying the possibility that there is a grounding truth.

* * *

As I said a moment ago, you can find arguments against absolute starting points for our knowledge of the world as far back as you care to go. According to Plato, Protagoras asserted that man is the measure of all things (*Theaetetus*, 152a): everything is relative to the human, and the human itself is conditioned by the surrounding world; and so there is no supra-human, context-free, way of determining the truth. In modern times those anti-foundationalists who have matured in the European literary and philosophical tradition look back to Friedrich Nietzsche as the first and most forceful advocate of their general position. In *The Gay Science* (1882; 1887) the Swiss philosopher included a vivid scene he had written about a madman. This strange character lit a lantern in the morning, Nietzsche says, then ran to the market and kept crying out, 'I seek God! I seek God!' The townspeople found this thoroughly amusing and mocked him, but the madman was in deadly earnest. God cannot be found, he tells them, because we have killed him. God is dead. The incomprehension of the townspeople shows that the madman has announced his message too early. He realizes that it will take a long time for the fact to sink in.

Exactly what it means to say 'God is dead' is far from clear. In itself it hardly counts as a scandal. After all, Christians believe that the second person of the Trinity became a human being and died for their sins. Some Lutherans still sing the hymn written by Johannes Rist in the mid seventeenth century that has the line 'Gott selbst liegt tot', 'God himself lies dead'. But Nietzsche's madman is not offering a remark about Good Friday, and doubtless Nietzsche takes him to be the only sane person in the market place. His madness is inspired. We need to work out, though, what it means to say that God is dead. Could the statement be no more than Nietzsche's testimony of atheism, his anguished cry that, alas, there is no God? If so, this is an odd kind of atheism, one in which God is held to have been alive once but has now passed away because of our lack of interest in him. Or could the statement 'God is dead' be a gnomic way of suggesting that genuine belief in the Bible has faded in modern times and that, while people still go to church, they live as though the transcendent world no longer had any determining power over them? This is a better interpretation. 'God is dead' would not be the strong assertion that the eternal God no longer exists but the weaker claim that Christian morality has become so compromised, so hypocritical, that Christians themselves act as though there is no God. Or, again, could it be that the formula has little or nothing to do with religious belief and is, rather, an elliptical way of saying that there is no absolute ground that will support our longing for the truth? If this interpretation is correct, Nietzsche is not offering a dismissive comment on the God of Abraham, Isaac and Jacob but is rejecting the God of the metaphysicians and moralists.

On balance, I think Nietzsche is denying that there is absolute being and is not making a specific statement about the non-existence of God. There is no grand metaphysical substructure that supports our knowledge of the world, he thinks, and any philosopher – Schelling or Hegel, say – who is credited with discovering one by a clever argument is sure to be mistaken. And yet any reader of *Twilight of the Idols* and *The Anti-Christ*, both written in 1888, will quickly see that Nietzsche seldom misses an opportunity to take a swipe at Christianity. One should not draw the distinction between the God of the prophets and the God of the philosophers too sharply when reading him. What we can say with confidence is that Nietzsche believed Christianity to be part of a long historical sequence that began with Plato and was ended by his own literary creation, the fiery prophet Zarathurstra who could never be mistaken as Christian or Jewish.

In his fable 'How the "Real World" Became a Myth', included in *The Twilight of the Idols*, Nietzsche traced the slow demise of the Western idea of a 'real world'. For Plato, the real world is the realm of the Forms; it can be reached by dialectical skill and wisdom. For Christianity, the real world is heaven: to gain entrance one must believe and wait. Later, for Kant, the heavenly world is not to be approached so much by faith as by morality: we can have no theoretical knowledge of the deity, and the best we can do is act morally, as though we knew there were a God. If we cannot know this so-called 'real world', Johann Gottlieb Fichte (1762–1814) announced, then it can surely have no claim upon us, not even by way of duty. Let us therefore abolish it. In doing so, however, we would not be left with an 'apparent world', for the distinction between 'real world' and 'apparent world' would break down. What intrigues Nietzsche, then, is not belief or non-belief in God so much as a process in the

Western philosophical tradition taken as a whole. The positing of a higher world, the abode of the Platonic Forms, as the supreme value for life unexpectedly set in motion the inevitable decline in the idea of value. This historical movement of devaluation is what he calls *nihilism*.

When people first come across anti-foundationalist arguments, especially of the 'God is dead' variety, they tend to respond fearfully by saying that this line of reasoning will undo all values and bring about an unholy mess of irrationalism, relativism and subjectivism. We need to maintain the Western metaphysical tradition if only to keep away from all those billowing clouds of mental fog. Better to read Aristotle or St Thomas Aquinas or even David Hume than Nietzsche, Foucault and Derrida! If Nietzsche could respond to this objection he would point out two things. First, he would say that nihilism does not call for a denial of values but instead requires us to revalue all our values. And second, nihilism is not opposed to metaphysics but is its hidden logic and consequence. In a fragment most likely written in 1887 or 1888, and now included in the unfortunately titled posthumous collection *The Will to Power* (1968), he suggested that the meaning of nihilism is that the question 'why?' cannot be answered. To give an answer to that question would be to supply a ground, and nihilism has eroded all grounds.

In a series of lectures on Nietzsche delivered in 1940 Heidegger wrested Nietzsche's fragment on the meaning of nihilism to his own concerns about the nature of being. Taking seriously Nietzsche's belief that nihilism implies a revaluation of all values, Heidegger argued two lines simultaneously. First, he contended that we cannot think value outside the sphere of being: a value is what is valid, and validity is the manner in which a value *is*. And second he proposed, more simply, that the very idea of 'value' implies a hierarchy: some values are higher than others. What then is the highest value? Plato held before us the Form of the Good, which was beyond being; Aristotle pointed to the Unmoved Mover; and Plotinus affirmed the One beyond Being. In the patristic age these ideas were used to make sense of the early Christian experience of God. St Clement of Alexandria and Origen, St Gregory Nyssa and St Augustine: all of them, along with many others after them, drew on the rich heritage of Greek thought to explain Christianity to themselves and others. For them there could be only one answer: God is the highest value because the deity transcends everything that is. No sooner is this answer allowed to orient how we regard God, Heidegger thought, than the slow process that will eventually degrade divine transcendence begins. The statement 'God is dead' means that absolute transcendence has lost all its authority and mystique. There are no metaphysical ends or ideals to which we can point that can satisfy and sustain us. We cannot determine a ground outside the immanence of ordinary human experience: not in divinity, and not even in a special region of humanity, such as consciousness. Christendom is thoroughly contaminated with nihilism, Heidegger declared, although an authentic Christian faith in God, which occurs outside all positing of values, is not. For those without faith, the only way out of this dire situation is to do what metaphysics cannot do, namely think its origin and thereby attempt to recover the meaning of being.

Nietzsche himself responded differently to the nihilism that he had diagnosed. We have lost the 'real world' and the 'apparent world', he thought, and it follows from this eerie situation that there are no facts, only interpretations. With that breathtaking claim we broach the doctrine that Nietzsche called 'perspectivism'. It is a shorthand for a group of different doctrines – that truth is perspectival, that logic is, that knowledge is, and so on – and this should be kept in mind when reading the philosopher. There is no absolute, Nietzsche declared: being is always becoming, and 'being human' is fluid rather than fixed. What counts as being moral has certainly changed as we have moved from the Classical to the Christian age; the meaning of the concept 'good' has shifted. Once it suggested nobility and strength; now it implies submission and weakness. There is no unconditioned ground to reality – no absolute perspective, no God's eye view of the world – only a plurality of forces that form themselves into groups, break apart and reform in other combinations. Each constellation of forces interprets the others in a robust sense of 'interpret', one that comes from a possible etymological source of the word – *pretium* or value. To interpret is to negotiate value. With no overarching meaning to be ascribed to the world, everything that happens is ultimately innocent. This is not intended in the negative sense that no experience, guilt or sin can be attached to people but in the neutral sense that the ethical statements one makes about actions are neither true nor false. And yet Nietzsche also believed that each force is affected by what happens to it; it gains more life, stays the same or loses life. There is no signification that is not also an evaluation.

Is Nietzsche contradicting himself? Because he does not write in a systematic manner, putting forward his views and defending them against possible objections, he is always vulnerable to appearing inconsistent. Of course, he writes in that way because he wishes to embody the perspectivism he endorses. Hence his volumes of aphorisms and fragments: *Human, All Too Human* (1878), *Daybreak* (1881), *The Gay Science* (1882) and *Beyond Good and Evil* (1886). And hence too the many other genres and styles in which he writes: the lyric, the fable, the essay, the parody, the genealogy, the autobiography, the harangue, the prophecy and the rhapsody. Not that Nietzsche's writing is directly a consequence of his adopting a theory of perspectivism. It must be remembered that, at his best, he is one of the nineteenth century's preeminent literary stylists. His predilection for writing aphorisms and fragments, for memorably saying in a few sentences what most philosophers would take hundreds of pages to say in a forgettable manner, converged with the theory of knowledge to which he bound himself.

Thinking of Nietzsche as a writer helps us to understand him as a philosopher. We do not have to go far in that direction, though, to excuse him from the charge of self-contradiction. As Arthur Danto pointed out in his pioneering study *Nietzsche as Philosopher* (1967), we can distinguish the philosopher's first-order views (his specific moral judgments) from his second-order views (his position on the *nature* of moral judgments). Nietzsche rails against the men and women of his day, telling them in no uncertain terms that they are frequently wrong to act as they do, and commending nobility and strength to them. And he also holds, as a theory of ethics, that moral judgments are neither true nor false. The position is a sophisticated one, and maybe difficult to maintain, yet it is not self-contradictory.

* * *

Perspectivism might be a consequence of nihilism but is plainly not co-ordinate with it. It does not rest content with the erosion of all values but aggressively seeks to revalue all values. How that revaluation is to occur is far from obvious. If we are not allowed to measure an interpretation against a fact, how can we judge whether the interpretation in question is fitting or not? And in the case of rival interpretations, how can we be sure that they are considering the same thing, if 'thing' makes any sense at all in this context? Nietzsche's answer is twofold. First, everything is always and already interpreted; we can never hope to lay our hands on a raw fact, a 'given' untouched by value. And second, some interpretations are stronger than others: they account for more meaning and give more meaning to life.

On this understanding, Nietzsche rejects the distinction between *interpreting* texts (in the sense of getting them right or wrong) and *using* them (to do philosophy oneself, to compose poems, to engage in politics, to get over a failed relationship). It is this aspect of Nietzsche's thought that attracts a contemporary pragmatist like Richard Rorty (1931–). There are no limits to interpretation, he tells us, because the distinction between what something really means and what I can do with it has become merely academic. Thinking about the true meaning of a text is part and parcel of essentialism, and rather than keep arguing against true meanings – and thereby keeping essentialism in play – it would be better just to change the topic. What is interesting is not whether an interpretation is *true* but whether it *works* in ways that a culture thinks valuable (to promote justice, to make art, to make people happy). Not all postmodernists are at ease with this highly consequent form of pragmatism. Umberto Eco, whose novel *The Name of the Rose* is, as you heard the other day, one of the icons of postmodernism, disagrees sharply with Rorty. His case is commonsensical. There must be limits to interpretation, he figures, otherwise a murderer such as Jack the Ripper could justify his acts by reference to his reading of the Gospel of Luke. And something else is implied as well. Unless we attend to the true meaning of a text we will have no basis to challenge the interpretations proposed by others. We will have no solid resources of critique available to fight against what oppresses us and other people.

Nietzsche's perspectivism affirms a plurality of force centers. What is important for Nietzsche, however, is not plurality so much as affirmation. It is *affirmation* that is to be affirmed, he tells us. We glimpse here a thought that has been widely adopted by postmodernists: 'double affirmation' or 'non-positive affirmation'. We can affirm life without positing an external origin or end to it. That life, that endless process of becoming, is *itself* an affirmation. Jacques Derrida has inherited this outlook from Nietzsche, and his detractors, who are legion, are often quick to assimilate him to the style of anti-foundationalism associated with the declaration 'God is dead'. I think this is inaccurate. Although Derrida is indebted to Nietzsche, he owes less to him than many people suppose. The other day you heard a story about Derrida presenting a paper, 'Structure, Sign and the Discourse of the Human Sciences', at a conference at the

Johns Hopkins University in 1966. That paper concluded with a contrast between two styles of interpretation. One style is associated with Jean-Jacques Rousseau (1712–78): it is characterized by a longing to decipher the hidden truth about the world, to find the true origin from whence we came, and to restrict play. The other, leagued with Nietzsche, affirms play, does not seek an origin, and fails to balk at the limits imposed by humanism or metaphysics. (Needless to say, this is the Nietzsche of the 1880s, not the author of *The Birth of Tragedy* (1872).) In the late 1960s and even in the early 1970s Derrida, especially in Great Britain and the United States, was taken to support a Nietzschean idea of free interpretation, unencumbered by origin or end. Yet if you look at all closely at his closing remarks you can only shake your head and wonder how on earth people ever thought that. He plainly says that those two interpretations of interpretation are inextricably bound together, and that we cannot choose between them. If you like, all interpretation has to negotiate a ground and a non-ground. It is never entirely free.

Before Derrida arrived in Baltimore he had completed a short, powerful study of Edmund Husserl that was later to appear in English as *Speech and Phenomena* (1973). It is here, as well as in an earlier study of a single essay by Husserl, 'The Origin of Geometry' (1936), that we find Derrida's main argument against absolute foundations. Let me stress that it is an *argument*. Some analytic philosophers – people who work in the Anglo-American tradition that comes from John Locke and passes through Bertrand Russell and G.E. Moore, and from them to Willard van Orman Quine, Wilfred Sellars and others – are quick to say that postmodernists and post-structuralists do not argue in a rigorous manner. Depending on whom they are talking about, they can be right. Jean Baudrillard, for instance, does not offer anything like an argument for his view that in the postmodern age referents have, in effect, been replaced by signs; he is offering a bold redescription of social reality, not trying to plead a case about epistemic justification, and overstatement is one of his tools (one he uses a little too often, it must be said). Yet not all analytic philosophers are devoted to arguments. One of the most important of them all, Ludwig Wittgenstein (1889–1951), offers very little by way of standard argumentation in either his early or his late works. For the younger Wittgenstein in particular, a philosophical text should be an artwork, and no work of art bothers to defend its thesis as a philosophical article does. His *Tractatus Logico-Philosophicus* (1921) elaborates itself as a series of numbered fragments, and, while it is an original and powerful piece of philosophy, in some respects it shows more affinity with other high modernist works of art, such as T.S. Eliot's *The Waste Land* (1922), than with contemporary papers in the philosophical journal *Mind*.

Debates over which is the better, Anglo-American or European philosophy, have tended to be tedious and debilitating for all concerned. At any time there will be little creative philosophy and a mass of uncreative philosophy, and whether you read a little library featuring Rudolph Carnap and Hilary Putnam or one that stars G.W.F. Hegel and Martin Heidegger will not make you a jot more creative. It will simply fix the vanishing points in the plane in which you can be creative or uncreative in whatever you write. From some angles Derrida appears as a remarkably uncreative philosopher, while from others he seems a strikingly fecund and original one, and it is worthwhile to take a few moments to see why this is so. Let's consider one or two features of his reading of Husserl's essay 'The Origin of Geometry'. And in order to do so, let's consider an ideal object of the sort that Husserl had in mind when writing on mathematics: a right-angled triangle. Husserl maintains that we cannot rigorously distinguish between the constitution of a timeless, ideal object – a right-angled triangle, for instance – and the historical transmission of its mathematical law through textbooks and classes in mathematics. His reason is an appealing one: language preserves the sense of an ideal object and allows other people to gain access to it. Now Derrida agrees with Husserl that language helps to compose ideal objects. However, he thinks that the German philosopher is mistaken about how language works. Husserl thinks that writing preserves ideal objects in an exemplary way, and it is over the nature of writing that the two philosophers disagree. Husserl asserts that the contingency and materiality of writing can be bracketed, leaving only the pure possibility of embodiment. Yet Derrida shows that embodiment cannot be separated from contingency and materiality. The *meaning* of a right-angled triangle can never be grounded in a pure mental act and adequately preserved in language; it is always vulnerable to the dangers of contingency and catastrophe.

How? Well, imagine that a mathematician draws a right-angled triangle on a piece of paper. The image can always be lost, burned, buried or erased; it can always be cut into bits, soaked in water, inserted in an unforeseen and perhaps inappropriate context, or delivered to the wrong address. Notice that Derrida is not arguing merely that unexpected disasters can befall a piece of paper on which the triangle has been drawn. He is suggesting that the possibility of catastrophe is a structural component of the inscription of the triangle. Even triangles can be quoted out of context! Many children at Sunday school have been perplexed by their teachers drawing triangles on a board in order to explain the nature of the Trinity. And, more engagingly, the French poet Eugène Guillevic wrote a charming collection of lyrics called *Euclidiennes* (1967) that are spoken by geometrical figures, including three species of triangle. Needless to say, no amount of cutting or quoting will ever change the mathematical properties of a right-angled triangle; and Derrida makes no claim that it will. His point, rather, is that not even an ideal object like a geometrical figure can ground itself. It needs the contingency and materiality of writing in order to be transmitted to a new generation of mathematicians. And that contingency and materiality can always be used to expose the ideal object to risks and contaminations that neither Pythagoras nor any mathematician would have in mind.

I have given only a rough and ready impression of Derrida's argument, leaving out many subtleties in his analysis, but two things should be evident. First, it *is* an argument. It proposes a view, supports it in a logical manner, and both the conclusion and the reasoning can be inspected and debated. Second, it is an argument leagued with a close reading of Husserl's essay. Many philosophers have aimed to develop free-standing arguments, the conclusions of which will not depend substantially on anything written by other philosophers. Derrida twins an argument with a reading. Indeed, it is almost impossible to tell in his texts where the reading ends and the argument begins. His originality consists partly in his style (a doubling of commentary and argument), partly in his claims (that linguistic contingency is irreducible, for instance) and partly in the sheer inventiveness of his reading of philosophical and literary works. And yet, when viewed from another perspective, Derrida has little claim to be regarded as an original philosopher. You can think of philosophy as a rattle bag of issues: the nature of truth, the mind-body problem, the debate between realism and nominalism, the nature of mind, the reality or non-reality of time, whether there are natural laws, whether existence is a predicate, whether ethical remarks are cognitive or non-cognitive, and so on. Perhaps no philosopher with as good a claim to permanence as Derrida has contributed so little sustained work to any of these conversations.

'Actually, it's a good thing that he hasn't become that sort of philosopher,' Richard Rorty might quip. 'It would be better for everyone if some of those conversations were to dry up.' Philosophy must stop trying to think of itself as a science, devoted to discovering a grounding truth outside the human mind, Rorty thinks. It must stop thinking of itself as a neutral judge of all other disciplines, and take part in the conversations taking place. The American pragmatist thinks that the young Derrida, the author of *Speech and Phenomena*, was on the wrong path when he was attempting to devise rigorous arguments against permanent grounds. It is better simply to do something else, to redescribe reality rather than dispute the description offered by Descartes and Leibniz. So Rorty prefers Derrida's later work, like *Glas* (1974) and *The Post Card* (1980), where he finds more creativity and playfulness and less attention to finding a non-foundational foundation to Western thought: *la différance* or *la trace* or whatever it might be. Derrida himself will not accept this carving up of his work, or the imputation that some of his writing is more creative than other parts. Yet the attempt to capture some European philosophers – most notably Heidegger and Derrida – and turn them into pragmatists, has been one of the livelier aspects of the postmodern intellectual world, especially in the United States.

* * *

If we take anti-foundationalism as our guiding thread to postmodernism, we will find ourselves in the United States as often as in France. We will find ourselves talking about Richard Rorty and Stanley Fish (1938–) as well as Jacques Derrida and Michel Foucault. Yet we will also find ourselves talking about Willard van Orman Quine (1908–2000), Wilfred Sellars (1912–89) and Donald Davidson (1917–), none of whom strikes either himself or us as a postmodernist. I don't propose to talk for long about any of these eminent philosophers, and this is not the place to detail and weigh their arguments that get rather technical quite quickly. But we need to have a broad familiarity with one or two of their central ideas.

Wilfred Sellars is known as an anti-essentialist. For him, there are no Platonic ideas or mentalist 'meanings': the conceptual order should be inserted into the causal order. And he is known too as a vigorous defender of scientific realism. Yet over the years his name has become almost synonymous with anti-foundationalism. Consider the allusion to him in Daniel Dennett's hilarious *The Philosophical Lexicon*. The website consists of definitions of adjectives, nouns and verbs based on the names of prominent philosophers. Thus the definition of the noun *sellar*: 'A deep, dark place beneath a weighty edifice that lacks foundations'. Specifically, Sellars is associated with an attack on what he called 'the myth of the given'. What he finds implausible is the view that there is something given in experience that is independent of our beliefs and concepts and that could justify them. That there is such a 'given' is, he says, no more than a myth. Exactly what Sellars means by 'the given' is far from self-evident. Much of his attention in his ground-breaking essay 'Empiricism and the Philosophy of Mind' (1956) is devoted to rejecting the theory of logical atomism, the metaphysical view pro-pounded by Russell and the young Wittgenstein that sense data supply the building blocks of the universe. We might debate whether Sellars actually does more than attack logical atomism, and whether he is successful in that campaign; and we might wonder if other forms of givenness would survive his argument against logical atom-ism. But there is no doubting that he takes himself to have shown that no foundation for our beliefs is given to us in our experience of the world.

Another highly acclaimed and influential essay of the same period, one that goes in the same general direction, is Quine's 'Two Dogmas of Empiricism' (1951). Kant distinguished analytic and synthetic judgments, that is, he drew a line between those statements that are true by virtue of their form and those that are not. A syn-thetic statement tells us something because it joins together two unrelated items ('Mary Jane Smith is a good pianist'), while an ana-lytic statement is logically true – or can be translated into a logical truth – and gives us no information at all ('Mary Jane Smith is female'). The first dogma that Quine disposes of is the analytical-synthetic distinction: he rejects analyticity because he is convinced that the notion covertly relies on circular reasoning. And the second dogma is reduction to sense data: once again, there is no 'given' to which we can appeal. If Quine's arguments against the two dogmas are good ones, what will follow from them? There will no longer be a sharp distinction between speculative metaphysics and the natural sciences, he says, and we will have fewer reasons not to become pragmatists.

For Quine, living without the two dogmas means that we cannot match simple ideas to our experiences (as eighteenth-century empiricists like Locke and Hume thought) or our experiences to those sentences based on observation (as the logical positivists thought). In the brave new world of undogmatic empiricism the whole of our experience has to hook up with all of our ideas about the world. We have passed, he tells us, from grounding our beliefs on something indubitable in experience to our living with beliefs about the world not being firmly grounded at all: in other words, empiricism has been transformed into a holism. So for Quine our knowledge is a vast web of beliefs all of which can, in principle, be revised. Those beliefs towards the edges of the web tend to be the ones that we will adjust, while those close to the center of the web are unlikely to be revised. There is no statement in science that is completely and totally protected from being recast or replaced, for there is no statement that is supported by an extra-mental entity. And yet we should soberly recognize that physical facts are the least likely of statements to be adjusted or rejected. Quine is an anti-foundationalist in the strong sense of the word since for him there is no base for our knowledge outside our shared beliefs about the world. Yet some contemporary foundationalists who are prepared to accept a weaker sense of 'foundation' are happy to have the philosopher on their team on account of his placing of physical facts at the center of the web of belief. That sort of foundation is as good as we can get, and we need something to protect us from a thoroughgoing relativism.

In some respects the work of Donald Davidson appears merely to extend Quine's, while in others it seems to encompass and enclose it. Thus Davidson agrees with Quine that we can get along nicely without the two dogmas of empiricism, while adding that there is a third dogma – that there is a distinction between a conceptual scheme and empirical content – that we can do without as well. (Quine does not concur.) Davidson applauds Quine's investigations into radical translation, that is, translation undertaken without any knowledge of the unfamiliar language and without any assumptions about it. And he extends these investigations into a new project, radical interpretation, which invites us to ponder how we can make sense of someone's utterances from scratch. Yet in his later work especially, when he turns to the theory of meaning, Davidson develops a more sweeping philosophy than Quine is prepared to countenance, one in which language is no longer regarded as a medium in which people think and talk and write. As Richard Rorty points out in *Contingency, Irony, and Solidarity* (1989), Davidson's idea is of a language of pure surface: sentences relate to other sentences and not to meanings. Even metaphors, which are usually conceived in terms of depth, are for Davidson only surface oddities or irritants that are not of another nature ('figural', for example) than literal statements. In a bold statement Davidson declares that there is no such thing as a language (by which he meant 'language' as it has traditionally been understood). It is the sort of provocative remark that analytic philosophers associate with Derrida ('There never was any perception', 'There is nothing outside the text'); but Davidson's terse style of writing remains within the genre of the research paper and his range of references (Kant, Wittgenstein, Tarski and Quine, among others) constitutes a respectable canon within the canon of analytical philosophy.

One index of Davidson's radicality as a thinker is that it is difficult to slot him into the usual positions available in contemporary philosophy. He is not an essentialist in the sense that he believes there are 'meanings' outside the human mind, and he proposes that interpretation is indeterminate, that is, an event can be interpreted differently. But he argues forcefully against relativism and skepticism. He is not a foundationalist to the extent that he urges us to accept a thoroughgoing holism: meanings and beliefs are interdependent for him. And yet he affirms that meaning finds its structure only in a theory of truth. Finally, he is neither a realist nor an antirealist because he thinks that particular debate has been poorly set up and generates a misguided conversation.

The best image that I can summon as a way of leaving Sellars, Quine and Davidson is one that was bequeathed to us by the Austrian philosopher Otto Neurath (1882–1945). He said that we are all like sailors trying to rebuild a boat on the open sea. Now and then the boat springs a leak or gets rusty or becomes encrusted with barnacles. We can never get to a dock to do a thorough job of repair, and have to replace bits and pieces when and how we can. We don't always have the right planks, the appropriate strength of steel, or custom-fitted equipment. We do what we can. Neurath's image is of the philosopher who cannot find a firm ground on which to base his or her beliefs. Now and then our working system of beliefs needs to be altered, and we do what we can to make it hold water. We can only use what we have to hand, bits and pieces of a tradition and our own ingenuity, and that just has to do.

Hardly any analytic philosophers over the last fifty years have been foundationalists in any strong sense of the word, although, as we have seen, some have rallied to the call for a modest foundationalism. Those analytic philosophers who reject foundationalism in favor of a complete holism are close in principle to those postmodernist thinkers who style themselves as anti-foundationalists and either affirm the abyss or go pragmatist. What separates the rude analyticals from the cool postmodernists? An analytical or post-analytical philosopher will tell us that it is a matter of rigor and detail. Anti-foundationalism, it will be said, does not necessarily imply anti-humanism or anti-realism; and it seems that many postmodernists subscribe all too quickly to all three positions, in some shape or form, without worrying whether they contradict one another. A postmodernist might imply that his or her difference from the analyticals and post-analyticals is more a question of style ('Who would want to hang out with those nerdy boys in the Philosophy Department?'). Both groups of people might be taken with the image of Neurath's boat, and each might want to set the other group afloat in it without an oar.

Imagine yourself alive two or three hundred years from now. It might turn out that postmodernism was something thin and fashionable that lasted only for a little while in the late twentieth century and the first years of the twenty-first century. Or it might turn out that people only started to recognize in the late twentieth century that a violent change had occurred: they began to notice only then that modernity started to give way to postmodernity as early as the eighteenth century. It might be hard in the future for people to see easily why Quine and Davidson were on one side of a line and Derrida and Lyotard were on another. The *how* might well lead away from the *what* of postmodernism. Or again, it might turn out to be hard to see why people bothered with Quine and Lyotard when it was all too clear that the really innovative people were Davidson and Derrida. Or, then again, it might turn out that all these people were no more than forerunners to someone or a group who embodied the postmodern more fully than we can conceive at the moment. And of course it might also turn out that what we call philosophy seems, for those people in the future, akin to what we call theosophy or astrology.

further reading

Danto, Arthur. *Nietzsche as Philosopher*. New York: Macmillan, 1967, ch. 3.

Eco, Umberto (with Richard Rorty, Jonathan Culler and Christine Brooke-Rose). *Interpretation and Overinterpretation*, ed. Stefan Collini. Cambridge: Cambridge University Press, 1992.

Fish, Stanley. 'Anti-Foundationalism, Theory Hope, and the Teaching of Composition', in his *Doing What Comes Naturally: Change, Rhetoric, and the Practice of Theory in Literary and Legal Studies*. Oxford: Clarendon Press, 1989, 342–55.

Rockmore, Tom and Beth J. Singer, eds. *Antifoundationalism Old and New*. Philadelphia: Temple University Press, 1992.

Rorty, Richard. *Contingency, Irony, and Solidarity*. Cambridge: Cambridge University Press, 1989.

postmodern experience

Are there experiences that have become characteristic of postmodern times? Does postmodernism offer fresh understandings of 'experience'?

These are totally different questions. Yet if postmodernism is in any way a reflection on postmodern times they should engage each other at one or more levels. Before we even begin thinking about these questions, though, we need to take a moment or two to consider what would be involved in answering them. The first question asks us to consider that there are experiences that we might expect in postmodern life but not in modernity or premodernity. It certainly seems plausible. My grandparents had no contact with the Internet, with email, with mall culture, or hyper-reality in general. They had never heard of John Cage or Charles Bernstein, and they died before people started to use credit cards or there was any talk about globalization. I could safely say that they had no experiences that we would consider 'postmodern'. By the same token, neither they nor I have lived without capitalism, clocks and crowds. Their experience was modern, and mine has been a mixture of the modern and the postmodern. If we go back eight hundred years or so, we could settle on a range of experiences that, from our vantage point, would be called 'premodern'. Living in the one village all your life, following the rhythms of the seasons, being protected by the lord of the manor, having the Church permeate all you do and think: these things suggest that experience back then was organized quite differently from that in modern and postmodern times.

Now these three categories are quickly drawn, and the lines dividing them are wavy and broken. We should be careful not to imply that each period has a *Zeitgeist*, a spirit of the age, which essentially distinguishes it from other historical periods. There may be movements within modernity, for instance, that ask to be recognized as 'modern' but in ways that do not square with our usual working sense of modernity. These 'para-modernities', as we might dub them, might have as good a claim to our attention as a normative idea of modernity, if there is such a thing. So let us take the division of history into the 'premodern', 'modern' and 'postmodern' with a pinch of salt. Yet, thinking of our experiences of email, mall culture and hyper-reality, and how they differ from the experiences of our grandparents, we might venture the hypothesis that there are experiences that are peculiarly postmodern.

Without a doubt, the second question is implying something far more dramatic, namely that experience *itself* has changed in postmodern times. This is a puzzling idea, one that runs counter to some of our most deeply entrenched assumptions. For example, we might readily admit that rituals of courtship and marriage have changed over the centuries, and that people show love in different ways in different cultures; but we are loathe to admit that the experience of love itself has changed. All people, at all times and in all places, fall in love, we tell ourselves. At the same time we know that the ancient Greeks had several words that might be translated into English as 'love' and that a citizen of Athens might have loving relations with an adolescent boy as well as with his wife. That citizen would not be familiar with our notion of 'romantic love' or with our idea of an exclusive heterosexual relationship forming the center of a nuclear family. So perhaps the experience of love has varied over time. Has *experience* itself changed in its structure, however? Deleuze would tell us it has: now we do not look to a transcendent ground, such as consciousness, to determine it. We might approach the issue more cautiously by asking if, in postmodern times, our experience of the world is organized otherwise than in earlier times. Or we might ask if a new theory of experience is gradually being accepted, one that fits our being in the world better than earlier theories. For the purposes of coming to grips with this difficult topic, it will be easier if we begin by taking this second approach. The first approach will interest us later.

There have been many philosophies of experience, although few of their adherents have taken historical and cultural differences fully into account. Some people, most notably Aristotle (384–322 BCE), have thought of experience as what happens when memories of doing the same thing accumulate and are slowly distilled into principles. So we talk of an experienced teacher as someone who has been in the classroom for a good many years, has encountered a wide range of students, and has learned a variety of ways in which a subject can be taught. Other people, known as idealists, have considered experience by way of changes in a world of ideas. I am presented with feelings and sensations, but my consciousness shapes them into particular experiences by way of categories like cause and effect, or the grammar of the language I speak, or the judgments I make and the memories I have. Michael Oakeshott (1901–90) is a lucid modern representative of this school, as a reading of his study *Experience and its Modes* (1933) will quickly show. The foremost modern idealist, G.W.F. Hegel (1770–1831), developed a more dynamic philosophy of experience in his *Phenomenology of Mind* (1807). *Erfahrung* or experience is the exile and return, as mediated, of what was once supposed to be immediate to consciousness. Logic, nature and spirit are all encompassed in a vast and rich experience of mind or spirit. Others, less willing to grant consciousness such power, figure experience by way of what our senses tell us about the physical world. These are empiricists. For these people, the raw information given by the world to our senses counts as experience that is then processed by concepts. The eminent English empiricist John Locke (1632–1707) argues that these concepts are themselves derived from earlier experiences. Rationalists disagree: René Descartes (1596–1650), for example, maintained that these concepts come directly from the mind, not from the world. And in his critical philosophy, which responded to both empiricism and rationalism, Immanuel Kant (1724–1804) sided with the rationalists. Our knowledge of the world might begin with experience, he said, but it does not follow that it arises from experience.

Over the last four centuries, philosophers have converged on the vocabulary of 'subject' and 'object'. I am a subject and I engage with an object. The object might be 'out there', like a tree in a field, or it might be 'in here', a memory of sitting beneath that same tree or a desire to do so. Speaking quite generally, we might say that modern philosophers have taught in all manner of ways that the interaction of subject and object generates something we call 'experience'. Yet postmodernists commonly reject the modern notion of the subject or, at least, thoroughly rework it. The subject is decentered, they say;

it is merely the place from which a voice speaks; or it is constituted by the play of desires or by being brought before the laws of various institutions. And if postmodernists are right to rethink the primacy of the subject, the very idea of experience to which we have become habituated will have to be rethought. If experience itself has changed, then presumably knowledge also has been refigured: in its contents, in what we take it to be, or in how we organize the items we count as knowledge.

* * *

You can find the word 'postmodern' as far back as the 1870s, when it was used to describe artworks that came after impressionism, but the word starts to approach the cluster of meanings it has now only in the 1950s. Charles Olson uses it towards the end of a letter he writes from Black Mountain College, North Carolina, on October 20, 1951 to his fellow American poet Robert Creeley. He sees himself and his friends as examples of postmodern man, and their challenge, he thinks, is to free themselves from the metaphysics, mythologies and writings of the past. In essays such as 'Projective Verse' (1950) and 'Human Universe' (1951–52) Olson argued that we must remain answerable to the richness and roughness of experience and not abstract from it or reduce it to just one plane. That has happened, he thinks, in modern poetry. The writer's experience has been truncated so that it fits into a settled voice and a stable sense of self; its contradictions and excesses have been sheared away so that it fits into a predetermined shape such as rhyming couplets, the sonnet, or even blank verse. The modern poem is closed: it dryly harmonizes all its parts, neatly resolves its paradoxes and balances its tensions. If we abandon set forms and write projectively, attending to our breath and the music of each phrase, we will be able to present experience on several planes at once. The poem will not be poured into a set form, like claret into a wine glass, but will exist as a field of tensions. Postmodern poetry, he implies, will not be oriented around a sovereign subject; it will not be the lyrical effusions of celebration or melancholy that one finds in William Wordsworth or John Keats. Rather than being inward and meditative, the postmodern poem will be energetic and exploratory.

Olson's thoughts about postmodern man were fragmentary at best, and his poetry, especially his major work *The Maximus Poems*

(1960–75), has not worn well. One thing we can retain from his theory and his practice is that postmodern experience is leagued with experiment. His modernist mentor, Ezra Pound (1885–1972), would have agreed, and their concurrence reminds us that here, as elsewhere, we should be careful not to draw a sharp line between modernism and postmodernism. I will have something to say about the conjunction of experience and experiment in a moment. Before then, though, we need to look at the word itself.

If we follow its etymology we will find ourselves all too quickly in a tangle. 'Experience' derives from the Latin *experiri*, which means 'to test' or 'to try'. The prefix *ex* means 'out of' or 'away from'. Our word 'experience' would therefore signify something like 'what we gain from trying or testing something'. We can go into more detail, though. The radical of the Latin word is *periri*, which can also be found in *periculum*, 'danger' or 'peril'. Going back beyond Latin to Greek, we find *peras*, 'limit', *pera*, 'beyond' and *peirô*, 'to cross'. It begins to look as though our word 'experience' draws from both danger and crossing over; and since crossing a border often involves some peril the two sources are not at odds with one another. So the word 'experience' perhaps means having come out of danger, having survived the risk of peril. If you trust etymological arguments, you might say that the English word 'experience' tells us something about how the English view experience: it is something that has occurred. 'We've had some experience, thank you, and we don't want any more!' I'm joking, of course, but all the same it is worth our while to look across the English Channel and see what happens there.

Germans today have two words for experience, *Erlebnis* and *Erfahrung*. The former denotes 'lived experience', encounters with people or things that we internalize by way of memories. The latter is the more general word for experience, the older word, and the one that Hegel used. Should we trace its etymology by way of *fahren*, 'to transport', or *fara*, 'danger'? It is not clear, and the best we can do is to say that *Erfahrung* carries the sense of exposing oneself to risk. If the word differs at all from the English *experience*, it is only in that it suggests going through a danger, not having come out of one. The French also distinguish lived experience from experience in general by using the words *vécu* and *expérience*. They use the one word, *expérience*, for both 'experience' and 'experiment'; and some of their writers who have been brought into the postmodern fold, perhaps with all manner of reservations, play on this. Georges Bataille explores the two facets of the word in his *Inner Experience* (1943) while Michel Leiris straddles the literature of experience and literature as experiment in his *Scratches* (1949), and both draw deeply from the surrealists' interest in the ambiguity.

Out of the French writers who talk about *expérience* I would like to take Maurice Blanchot (1907–2003) as our companion. He was a friend of both Bataille and Leiris, and was sympathetic to the surrealists. Younger French philosophers also draw from his speculations. I think in particular of Philippe Lacoue-Labarthe's *Poetry as Experience* (1986) and Jean-Luc Nancy's *The Experience of Freedom* (1988). Blanchot's fundamental ideas achieved their first maturity in the 1940s, towards the end of what is conventionally called the modern era, although he and his friends – Georges Bataille and Emmanuel Lévinas, in particular – have become touchstones for many who style themselves postmodernists. Narratives such as *Thomas the Obscure* (1941) and *Death Sentence* (1948) are not commonly listed in guides to postmodern fiction, although they could feature there. As with Samuel Beckett's narratives, Blanchot's at once partly exemplify and greatly exceed what is usually offered under the banner of the postmodern. So far as I know, Blanchot never spoke of postmodernism or postmodernity, but it is hard to imagine post-structuralism without him. His influence on Deleuze, Derrida and Foucault was far-reaching and varied. And, as we shall see, one of the main ideas of postmodernism can be traced directly to him.

Blanchot's entire work, his criticism and his narratives, broods on *expérience* and does so in a profound way. In an essay on Michel Leiris that appeared in 1947 he declared that the point of writing is not self-expression but meeting risks that will change the writer. This process of change is far from straightforward: Blanchot insists that the experience literature makes available is essentially deceptive, and that its value is constituted in that. How is literature deceptive? In many ways, but consider this example. A writer might be perfectly sincere when composing a poem and it might show, yet his or her sentiment can end up appearing comic when read by another. (As André Gide sharply noted, all bad literature is made of fine sentiments.) Another writer might be insincere, doing no more than following a convention when composing, yet he or she might be praised for the authenticity of what is offered to the public. In writing, one can lose certainties that seemed to be firmly in place before picking up a pen. Writers frequently tell stories about having learned from their writing. 'Before I wrote that story, I thought I believed in happy endings,' a novelist might say, 'but in following my characters right to the end I realize that I am not as optimistic as I thought I was.' (In outline, the claim is not a new one: St Augustine testifies in one of his letters that he comes upon new ideas only by writing.) Also, Blanchot thinks, in writing one can discover something that it is impossible ever to lose. One can risk finding oneself placed in relation to that which has no meaning and no world. It is this eerie thought that preoccupied him over his long life, and one that we need to understand. We can best do so by examining his theory of the imaginary.

Literature begins as a quest for the real, but no sooner has the quest commenced than the real withdraws. I begin to write a poem about a stone resting on my desk, for example, and none of my words, not even any arresting metaphors I might invent, capture the thing. To be sure, my poem becomes an image of the stone, and following a long tradition I tell myself that in this image I have, to a greater or lesser extent, captured the truth of the original. On this classical understanding of art, the image is maintained at a distance from what I am writing about. Yet Blanchot insists that the stone is always and already able to be experienced as an image. In the moment in which I apprehend the stone, I seize not the stone itself but an image of it. The relationship between the thing and the image is what Blanchot calls 'resemblance', and he situates this relationship in being.

When a stone appears before me it is at once itself and an image of itself, and this image can repeatedly be detached from the stone. This possibility of the image to be detached from the thing is hidden when we conceive the image along classical lines. We might say that the classical image shields us from something disturbing. For we are at home with the image as traditionally understood: it gives us a meaning and a truth. But we are not at home with the relationship of resemblance, since we cannot grasp it and in no way does it reassure us with a meaning or a truth. Rather than consoling us with the thought that the real and the image are distinct and stable orders, that we can measure the truth of the image against the real, it tells us that the imaginary is within a thing, or, if you like, that the distance *between* a thing and its image is always and already *within* the thing. It is none other than *being* that subverts any attempt to compare the real and the imaginary.

An artwork turns on an ambiguity that can never be resolved, Blanchot argues. On the one hand, it offers us meaning and truth: we read a poem about a stone and can make decent sense of it. It tells us something memorable about the stone, and we are at ease because the image gives us a certain mastery over nature. We have comprehended the stone with our imaginations, and the poem now holds the stone at a distance. On the other hand, we see that the poem opens onto another space, one in which no firm distinction can be drawn between 'stone' and 'image of the stone'. We lose our grip on the real; we have no sway over the movement of resemblance because it has always been in train. Rather than holding an image at a distance from the real, we are held by the distance within reality. To read the poem on the stone is to pass from image to resemblance, from meaning to non-meaning, or, as Blanchot likes to say, from the possible to the impossible. We must learn to speak two languages, he tells us, one that is attuned to the possible and another that is a response to the impossible.

Blanchot gives several names to where this movement of resemblance points us: the outside, the imaginary, the neutral, and of course the impossible. To be led towards the outside is to lose all sense of security in oneself as a coherent self. Why? Because, following Hegel, Blanchot thinks that the 'I' is a power of negation. I maintain myself as a subject by negating the world, by having a dialectical response to it, and when I cannot do that I am no longer able to sustain myself as a self. Let's continue with the example we have been considering. In writing a poem about a stone I might well begin in quest of the real. I negate it in order to make discrete images: I ponder the darkness of the stone before me and write 'a starless night'. Soon, though, I am confronted not by a safe distance between my image and what I am representing but by a distance, a relentless withdrawal that has always and already started, within the real itself. I do not gaze at the impossible, for there is nothing there; rather, I am gripped in its dark gaze. Nothing *happens* in the outside; it is not 'another world' placed alongside this one. It could never become the subject of an episode in 'The Twilight Zone', for example. To discern its approach, however fleetingly, is to be exposed to a stagnant nonplace where nothing begins or ends. Far from being a space of death, which could at least console one with the thought of non-existence, it is the space of an endless dying where one is condemned to wander endlessly. For the Blanchot of *The Space of Literature* (1955), the writer is the one who discerns the approach of this horrible space and, unable to negate it and thereby turn it into an image, loses the power to say 'I'.

For Blanchot, the writer is exemplary in passing from the first to the third person, from being an 'I' to being a 'one'. Michel Foucault was vitally impressed by this insight, and held Blanchot to be a prime witness to a historical mutation, a new *episteme* – that is, a way in which our knowledge is organized – that would be characterized by the erasure of the human subject. One sign of this new *episteme*, which Foucault believes to be slowly dawning around all of us, is regarding literature as *expérience*. We can see it, Foucault says in *The Order of Things* (1966), in the writings of Stéphane Mallarmé and Franz Kafka and, with special force, in Blanchot's narratives and criticism. The valuable experiment these writers have been performing, each in his distinctive way, is to cease orienting themselves with reference to 'I think' and to take 'I speak' as a reference point, even though each of them construes the speaker as disappearing from the scene of writing. To engage in this experiment, Foucault believes, is to come to terms with the approach of what Blanchot called the outside. We might think of this new *episteme* as the postmodern age. Many things might be involved in coming to terms with it, but one central element will be a refiguring of 'experience'.

How can we distinguish modernity and postmodernity? Here is one way. Let us assume that modernity asks us to conceive a distance between reality and image, presence and representation. Experience will therefore involve some mastery over the world, the assertion of the 'I' with respect to nature. Now let us assume that postmodernity discerns the relationship of resemblance, a withdrawal of being at the heart of the real itself. There can be no controlling of reality here, and the 'I' will lapse into a neutral 'one'. Doubtless postmodern men and women will still seek meaning and truth, although they will also be aware, uneasily so, that being itself undercuts the possibility of meaning and truth. The outside is not an alternative to being; it is a split in being. Such is the message that Blanchot and Foucault join to tell us.

* * *

An artist, Blanchot tells us, is someone who lives an event as an image. When an ordinary man looks outside his bedroom window after getting home from work and sees the snow thickly falling on a black tree all he perceives is the garden, the tree, and the snow. If the man's wife is an artist, and she comes up behind him and looks over his shoulder, she will detach the image from the phenomenon. She does not have to paint a picture of what she sees or write a poem about it. Simply by looking through the window she will have experienced the snow falling on the tree *as an image*. For the woman, the event is already an image. It is not simply an image of an event; rather, it is an event that occurs: the woman is pulled toward the point from which the image derives, and in doing so she loses full possession of herself as a sovereign self. She might say, 'It's like being inside Robert Frost's poem "Stopping by Woods on a Snowy Evening"' or she might think to herself, 'It has the feel of Pieter Bruegel's painting "The Hunters in the Snow"', or it might inspire her to play some notes on the piano. What interests Blanchot is that the artist discerns that the real *already* has a quality of being a poem or a painting or a chapter in a story. When an artist looks at the snow falling on the black tree, time has already stalled. She is gripped in a state of fascination: not by the snow falling on the tree but by the outside.

The same thing happens in a work of art. Time does not flow ever onwards in a poem or a painting. In Robert Frost's poem the speaker is always stopping before the snowy woods, his little horse is always shaking his reins, and the speaker always has to go on with his journey. He never arrives anywhere, just as he never leaves from anywhere. To read that poem, Blanchot would say, is a threefold process. At first the reader is active, trying to make sense of it; then one is passive, learning from it; and finally one lets oneself be taken captive by the image that it is, held in a state of fascination. As we read and reread the poem, its language does not disappear into its use. Instead, it appears all the more forcefully as rhythm and rhyme. Here language is not used as an instrument, as when I tell someone 'Go outside and shovel the snow on the driveway', but is allowed to idle. To the extent that the poem is image, it does not offer itself to be used. Which is not to say that, in other circumstances, the poem cannot be put to work: a teacher can always read students 'Stopping by Woods on a Snowy Evening' in order to teach them about meter and rhyme or moral responsibility or North American perceptions of nature. As Blanchot says, and as we have already heard, we must learn to speak in two languages, one that names the possible and another that responds to the impossible.

When we are drawn into Robert Frost's poem, when we encounter it as image, we cannot say that we stand before it as an object. The image has withdrawn into itself, and there is nothing to stand before. So if we are moved to speak of experience here, we must do so only with a serious caveat. For Blanchot is urging us to accept that, in encountering art in this way, we have an experience of non-experience. No longer is there a distinction to be discerned between 'subject' and 'object', and consequently there can be no 'experience' in the usual sense of the word. Yet Blanchot introduces another distinction: the encounter does not happen, it occurs. There is no time, as we count it on the clock or even within ourselves, in which we can experience an image. Blanchot will tell us, especially in *The Writing of the Disaster* (1980), that non-experience has the same defining trait as experience. That is, we are exposed to the possibility of danger. The peril, as he sees it, is none other than recognizing that the division we usually take to be between being and image is within being itself.

Who knows that? First of all, as we have seen, the artist who experiences the event as image; but also, as Blanchot came to see in the 1960s, ordinary people such as the artist's husband. He may not experience an event as image, but he vaguely understands that the everyday escapes any and all categories. To experience everyday life, he recognizes, is to live in a world not organized by a subject and where there is no object. It is a neutral world in which nothing truly happens, only gossip and rumors that have no origin, a world that has never commenced and that will never end. One emblem for the grayness of the everyday might be a worker on an assembly line. Another might be the world depicted in the TV serial 'Seinfield' where, famously, nothing ever happens. If nothing begins in the everyday, it is because things just begin over again. Everyday life is the time of repetition. No one has ever had lived experience of the everyday, for our lives are spent in not experiencing it. Our everyday lives – driving on the freeway, lunching in the diner, filling in forms, picking up the children from school, making dinner, watching a movie – are not so many experiences so much as the absence of experience. In everyday life, Blanchot tells us, there is no truth or falsity, no subject or object, no beginning and no end. We are approached by the outside.

Postmodernists have learned two important lessons from Blanchot, although they have often got them second- or third-hand. The first lesson largely defines being postmodern. It is not that *representations* of reality are flawed in one way or another, but that reality *itself* is ontologically insecure. And the second lesson, closely related to the first, is that postmodern men and women, boys and girls, experience the real as image. As we have seen, we can put that more forcefully: to the extent that we are postmodern and give ourselves over to experiencing the world as image we no longer have experience. Of course, one can convict Blanchot of nostalgia. We can say that watching a DVD in the evening is every bit as much an experience as being slapped in the face or making a horseshoe. 'I sat before the screen,' someone will say, 'and I saw images that gave me pleasure and sometimes a little pain.' And then that same person might say, perfectly reasonably, 'and surely that was an *experience*'.

A convinced postmodernist would reply that you were confusing experience with a trait that is common to experience and non-experience. Or, if you like, the evening you spent with the DVD was only a more intense version of your day. All morning and all afternoon you were consuming images: McDonald's and Coca Cola, Shell and AT&T, billboards advertising underwear by Calvin Klein and radios broadcasting pop music, your colleague's new Armani suit, that joke at lunch about Lake Woebegone, and the fragrance worn by that woman down in Accounting, not to mention the images on your computer at work, the email you received and sent, the search engines you used, and the various websites you visited. Your whole day was an experience of non-experience. What did you hold onto when watching that DVD? Perhaps you were trying to make sense of it. Fine: but you knew that you had no mastery over that image, didn't you? You knew that you were responding to an image, not a firm reality, and if you had given yourself over to the image – perhaps it was the umpteenth time you had watched *Casablanca* – you would have been utterly passive, happy to have vanished into images that appear only to have no use at all: a gesture of Humphrey Bogart's hand, a look of tenderness in Ingrid Bergman's eyes.

* * *

To live reality as an image is to live in what many postmodernists call hyper-reality. We live in a world of images that seem more real than the natural world about us. Birds seen on digital TV are more intensely colored, more sharply defined, than those same creatures outside in the woods. The prefix 'hyper' also suggests something we are already beginning not to notice: postmodern life is a state of being perpetually over-stimulated. Desire is no longer something we feel from time to time; it has become the medium in which we live and move and have our being. Postmodern men and women know very well the experience of insufficiency: it is what fuels their zest for adventure, their reluctance to make commitments, and their ability to remake themselves. In thinking along these lines we have quietly passed from pondering a new theory of experience to thinking of experiences that are characteristic of postmodernity.

In North America and Europe, in particular, our experience of the world as image has taken on an aesthetic dimension. We view the world as spectators, enjoying or being struck by events that are set before us. The privileged fly from city to city, whether for work or recreation, and have become a new kind of tourist. No longer are they tourists for a few weeks each year; their entire lives are structured by it: there is recreational tourism, of course, but also employment tourism, information tourism, sexual tourism and cultural tourism. A holiday might consist of a flight to the Bahamas, and a good time will have been had if it accords more or less with the images of having a good time that are displayed in the booklets one reads before deciding on that destination. Work will involve going to conferences in desirable cities, and perhaps in other countries, where you hear talks by key people in the profession. They are viewed as 'star performers' or, in the academy, as 'star professors'. Perhaps you need to take another course in order to be promoted. Chances are you will surf the web, looking at suitable institutions, and will enroll in a course that can be delivered on-line to you at home or in the office. The borders between work and leisure have become increasingly divided and equivocal for the professional classes.

On Saturday morning you walk around the mall, looking for another pair of shoes or a winter jacket. If you stay longer than you imagined you would, perhaps having coffee or lunch, it is partly because you are a tourist there. You don't have to go to France or Italy or Japan. They have been brought to your hometown as a series of carefully produced images. So the world is held before you for your pleasure, assuming, of course, that you have the income or the appropriate level of credit. Tourism used to be based on an idea of authenticity: 'Next summer I will go to Athens and actually stand in the Parthenon, and I will go to Rome and really walk around the Colosseum ...' Now, in its extended sense, tourism is based on something that appears beyond the distinction between the authentic and the inauthentic: the image. No one goes to Disneyland in order to have an authentic experience, to perceive the 'aura' of the place. You go there to enjoy images that have no ground in reality, to spend money and to have fun. And increasingly London, Paris and Rome are not so different in people's imagination from a holiday in Disneyland. This fun comes at a price, however. As Julia Kristeva (1941–) warns in *Intimate Revolt* (1997), our imaginative life is being quickly eroded by constant exposure to the new technologies of the image. This is not a matter of responding to art with the passivity that Blanchot believes to be the final stage of an adequate response. It is a matter of becoming inert, sluggish and uncritical.

There are yet darker tones to tourism in its postmodern phase. A war is declared, and when you watch the news on TV you see elegant bombs that cost immense sums destroying buildings or arms factories. It is an aesthetic experience: those explosions are beautiful, like fireworks, and that collapsing building is quite sublime. The TV network's diagrams of how the missile is launched, and their information about how accurate it is: well, all that is more absorbing than watching 'Star Trek' or *Star Wars*. To think that this is actually happening! That is a buzz that the channel of your choice could not pay good money to show. Jean Baudrillard wrote a book entitled *The Gulf War Did Not Take Place* (1995), and it was much discussed. Or rather, I should say that the *title* was much discussed and the book was not widely read. 'How awful Baudrillard is,' some people said at the time, 'to deny that the war took place.' (The sentiment was shared by folk on the left and on the right of politics.) 'It shows just how heartless those postmodernists are.' (Again, the judgment was uttered, in almost the same words, by both the left and the right.) Could it be that at least one prominent postmodernist was so crazy as to suggest that a war that killed so many people never took place?

The short answer is 'No'. The longer answer would fall between yes and no, and it would incorporate a response, apologetic or not, about Baudrillard's choice of title, and, more generally, his tendency to over-statement. We are hostages of the media: that is one of Baudrillard's theses, and if he is right we are comfy hostages indeed, being well fed, having comfortable beds, and not being tortured. Stripping the rhetoric from the thesis, Baudrillard's point is relatively clear. Newspapers, TV and current event programs hold us captive in their presentation of what is happening. The news is not a transparent medium that communicates the facts, Baudrillard argues. Not at all: it creates illusions, 'reality effects', or what he calls simulacra. What the media gave us, he argues, is hyper-real simulacra of the war, not what 'really happened'. One of the illusions was that a war was going on. But if the bombing of Iraq occurred with the approval of the United Nations, it could not be a 'war' in the usual sense of the word, merely a military operation. What we are told on TV does not present what happens, Baudrillard says, it hides what is occurring; and it does so with a bombardment of information about the war. It will be objected that we *saw* events minutes after they happened, that we knew more about what was happening than at any other time in world history. Yet Baudrillard will reply that this too is an illusion. The reporting was highly selective, seen only through certain eyes that were credited in advance with the right to speak.

Did the Gulf War happen? Of course it did: men and women and children were killed or maimed. It was a wretched event, like each and every war, and, like all wars, it presents us with a contradiction. It should be investigated at every level and at every point so that we know what happened and in the hope that such things might be prevented; and yet, at the same time, commentary on it risks being offensive, and all the more so when it traffics with sophistry. The suffering of innocents should not merely be 'understood' – calibrated, measured, weighed – but denounced and lamented. Yet the question can be rephrased: did the 'Gulf War' happen? If one means by that, was the account of the war as given in the media a complete and accurate presentation of reality, then the answer is closer to no than to yes. We were given an impressive presentation of hyper-reality, as Baudrillard points out, although I very much doubt that the hyperreal completely hid the real. Even Baudrillard acknowledges that soldiers and civilians were killed in the war, that bombs destroyed or damaged buildings, and that large tracts of land were systematically burned by the Iraqi military.

There is a real behind the hyper-real, and we have come to a strange pass when one has to tease out of a thinker that nature and artifacts exist independent of images and our ability to manipulate them. How far we have come from the moral responsibility of Blanchot who, while convinced that reality is ontologically insecure, nonetheless denounced the cruelty and barbarity of the bombing of Baghdad. He was not alone. Many people who watched the Gulf War on TV were ravaged by images of human suffering in Iraq. For them it was not a spectacle; it was a window onto reality. This woman's face shows pain: *something has happened, it is real and it must be stopped*. Baudrillard's countryman, Luc Boltanski, calls this reaction *souffrance à distance*, and we have yet to gauge the effects that it is having on us. Baudrillard is on more solid ground when he argues that no story is ever the whole story. To the extent that the Gulf War was represented only from some perspectives, viewpoints that had at their command extraordinary powers of visual persuasion, that complicated event was not adequately covered. That is one of Baudrillard's points, another one being that it was not possible, given that the media speak from far within the Western, Judeo-Christian tradition, to give a comprehensive account of what happened.

Baudrillard's deep concern about the ability of the American and European media to stage-manage anything, even a war, is one that we should share. To be vigilant readers of the news and current affairs is a cardinal virtue in our intellectual and political lives; and to know how to read is a necessary ground of that, something that the formal study of literature can teach us. Baudrillard did not deny that Americans and Iraqis were killed in January 1991, but his analyses remained at the level of the image and the sign; and once we translate his fancy vocabulary into ordinary language his claims are not hard to accept. Yet we see that they are partial truths, blown up to full, or overfull, truths. Like a balloon you fill too energetically with hot air, a truth that is made with too much rhetoric will surely burst.

* * *

When we think of postmodern men and women, we usually have in mind the privileged or at least the moderately well off and well educated. It is the professionals whose lives are organized more and more around the Internet and email, who rapidly consume images, and who can experience life as play. To be postmodern is to be successful, to be young or, if no longer young, to be able to recreate yourself. Our rough-and-ready idea of postmodern men and women gives us an image of rootless individuals, people who do not trust any sort of linear history. They treat the past as an archive from which they can select items at will, parody them or quote them out of context for a special effect. We think of people who are wholly absorbed in a world of tele-technology and digital information that did not even exist twenty years ago. Could it be that they are living in a world without history?

The prior question is this: Can history end? Alexandre Kojève thought so. In a series of important lectures on Hegel's philosophy of religion delivered at the École practique des Hautes Études in Paris from 1933 to 1939, he argued that history had more or less come to an end already, and we were merely awaiting the *dénouement*. Like Hegel, Kojève thought of history as the story of opposition, and he focused on Hegel's brilliant analysis of the struggle between the lord and the bondsman in the *Phenomenology of Mind* (1807). The lord has power over the bondsman but is diminished in his self-estimate by recognizing that his selfhood turns on a relation with an inferior. At least the bondsman sees self-consciousness in the lord and in his power of dispensing life and death, and his labor offers a more acceptable way of coming to terms with the material world than the lord's fleeting pleasures ever can. Through his labor, the bondsman realizes that he has a mind of his own; and he recognizes that his freedom lies in no longer having his sense of self being referred to the existence of a lord. The distinction between lord and bondsman must be overcome. Such is the basis of social revolution, as Karl Marx realized.

When there is no longer any conflict between the lord and bondsman, there will be no more war and therefore no more history. In the eighteenth and nineteenth centuries all the wars necessary for independence, freedom and human rights were fought and won. We think of the American Declaration of Independence (1776), the Declaration of the Rights of Man and of the Citizen (1789) and the American adoption of the Bill of Rights (1791). For Hegel, history had essentially drawn to a close with the triumph of Napoléon at the Battle of Jena in 1806. No longer would there be a conflict between lord and bondsman, he thought, for now all people would be equal citizens in a new, universal state. A convinced Marxist, Kojève recognized that Hegel had brought down the curtains on history before the last act had properly concluded. Only with the communist revolution in Russia had the final scene of human social evolution commenced, and when international communism could be achieved history would indeed come to an end. There would be new conflicts, doubtless, but they would be no more than disputes to do with territory or trade, not struggles that bore on the essence of being human. With history behind us, 'man', the old human subject, would be dead. We would be able to recreate ourselves as comrades in a new international order, and would be free to devote our energies to art and play, study and love.

This Marxist vision of the end of history (and, for Marx himself, the beginning of a truly *human* history) has been discredited for several generations now. Yet the allure of the end of history, and the arrival of a new sort of human subject, is still attractive for some people. To the surprise of many on the left wing of politics, Kojève's arguments were revived in a modified form in support of right-wing politics. I am thinking of Francis Fukuyama's book *The End of History and the Last Man* (1992). History has indeed come to an end, Fukuyama maintained, not through the victory of international communism but rather through the triumph of global capitalism. It is liberal democracy that points the way to a world without war, in which there will be only conflicts arising from trade. Only liberal democracy can be effectively globalized, and it can do so when pre-ceded by or quickly followed by a shift towards a free-market econ-omy. The Promised Land is not to come; it is essentially here in the liberal democracies of the world.

Fukuyama draws deeply from Jewish and Christian motifs, the Promised Land and the Kingdom, although no religious person in those traditions could be happy with the vision of God's promise being fulfilled in no more than the free market. The divine promise is for God to be definitively with his creation, not for some people to have ample material wealth while others starve and not for the natural world to be unbalanced by unregulated emission of gasses. The point is worth remarking. If postmodernity is leagued with late capitalism, as it surely is, we need to keep in mind that it has not simply altered how the financially secure live. It has influenced the entire world at every level and at almost every point. No one is untouched by the activities of the International Monetary Fund and the World Trade Organization, no one is unaffected by the destruction of the world's ecosystems by an over-stimulated industrial economy. The hole in the ozone layer over Antarctica may have gotten smaller in the last year, but the level of dangerous gasses directly above the hole has recently peaked. Nor is it at all certain that the multiplication of liberal democracies will prevent another world war. It is just as likely that globalization will be regarded as a profound and incessant threat to Islam, especially to its many fundamentalists; that it will be resisted by a new kind of warrior, the international terrorist; and that a badly managed confrontation between the United States and any one of a number of countries will escalate into nuclear war.

Jacques Derrida responded to Fukuyama in a lecture delivered at the University of California, Riverside, in 1993. It was later expanded to become *Specters of Marx* (1994). Among other differences between them, Derrida indicated that democracy should not be thought as fully present now or to be entirely embodied in a future present.

Instead, democracy is always to come. No matter how preferable our form of government is to what was possible a hundred years ago, or a thousand years ago, there is always a gap between what democracy is and what it can be. At the heart of democracy, Derrida argues, there is a promise. There will always be more to be drawn from the concept of democracy that we have inherited from Athens, from England, and from the United States. What we experience now is a determinate form of democracy, and doubtless we will wish to retain many of its elements. More elusively, we also experience a promise there as well, that the other, each and every other, will be respected and made welcome in our democracy.

This affirmation of the other does not imply that we invite known terrorists into our country and allow them to do whatever they like. Of course not: there must be procedures in place to prevent those with evil intent from entering a country. It means, rather, that when we play host to someone we do not know in advance what that person will do. He or she might well live with us, come to the view that our system of government should be modified, win support for that view and, in time, effect a transformation of the very democracy that attracted him or her in the first place. Democracy is not something that is merely passed on from one generation to another. We need to remind ourselves that at first democracy was thought exclusively in terms of fraternity: women did not have democratic rights. To give those rights to women transformed democracy. We need to recall that in some societies people of color have not always had full democratic rights. In Australia, for instance, the aboriginal peoples were not allowed to vote until the mid-1960s. In both those instances there was more to be drawn from the concept of democracy than had been thought desirable. Even now, when women and people of color have largely gained democratic rights, at least in the first world, there are challenges to democracy, new transformations that right now seem impossible but that might well impinge on us. For example, we can imagine a democracy that exceeds the limits of nationhood, and does not require people to become citizens of just the one nation state. To say 'yes' to democracy is to affirm what we have now. Derrida invites us to affirm that affirmation, to say 'yes' to the promise at the heart of democracy, and, in doing so, to recognize that, beyond the politics of the possible, democracy is always to come. Postmodern politics, on this understanding, is a long way from endlessly contesting political liberalism. It endorses it at several points, even while distancing itself from any assurance of social progress.

Is postmodernity a time at the end of history, a period in which there is no experience? I do not think so. There is more to be done to make our laws just. There will always be more to do, there will always be more of the promise of democracy to experience. Yet when sitting before the Internet all day and watching TV in the evening, it can sometimes seem as though history is a thing of the past.

further reading

Baudrillard, Jean. *The Gulf War Did Not Take Place*, trans. Paul Patton. Bloomington: Indiana University Press, 1995.

Blanchot, Maurice. 'Gide and the Literature of Experience', in *The Work of Fire*, trans. Charlotte Mandell. Stanford: Stanford University Press, 1995, 212–25.

Derrida, Jacques. *Specters of Marx: The State of the Debt, the Work of Mourning, and the New International*, trans. Peggy Kamuf, introd. Bernd Magnus and Stephen Cullenberg. London: Routledge, 1994.

Quasha, George, ed. *The Station Hill Blanchot Reader*. Barrytown: Station Hill Press, 1999.

the fragmentary

When reading philosophy or theology and feeling a little lost when things become complicated there is no better way of getting back on track than to ask the following question: Who or what is taken to be the enemy here? It sometimes happens that philosophers and theologians mistake their enemies; they are really arguing against someone they have not named or perhaps dare not name. If we take them at their word, most of the eminent postmodernists are arguing against some or all of 'totality' and 'unity', 'origin' and 'presence', 'essentialism' and 'realism', 'universalization' and 'homogeneity'. We can come to understand them by way of their arguments against these things, and of course we can try to make better sense of them by following what they are arguing for. At its most general, their answer is 'difference' and 'the fragmentary', 'simulacra' and 'trace', 'singularity' and 'heterogeneity'. Any of these could provide us with a suitable idea of what postmodernists affirm, but, at our stage of discovery, the fragmentary offers to take us the furthest in the shortest time. So I want to talk about the fragment and the fragmentary.

They are not the same thing, and we could not do better than to think that observation through to the end. We might start by acknowledging that we find fragments as far back as classical times. We talk of the fragments of Heraclitus, although we surmise that they are bits and pieces of a treatise he started to compose about 500 BCE. Quite different are the aphorisms traditionally attributed to the physician Hippocrates: pithy statements that could readily be memorized and recalled for later use. We all know the start of the first one: 'Life is short, art is long.' Different again are the epigrams of Callimachus (*c*.305–*c*.240 BCE) or Martial (*c*.40–*c*.104). They were not written as parts of a unity that was never achieved or has been lost. They are short poems complete unto themselves.

Now all these classical aphorisms, epigrams and fragments differ from the fragment, and the idea of the fragment, as developed by the Romantics many centuries later. Perhaps you remember Samuel Taylor Coleridge's poem 'Kubla Khan' with its visionary landscape of Alph, the sacred river, the stately pleasure-dome, and the sunless sea. In a note to the poem he tells us that, while excitedly composing it in 1797, he was disturbed by a person from the nearby town of Porlock who had some business to transact with him, and that when he returned to writing his poem he found he could not remember how it was to continue. So 'Kubla Khan' remained a fragment. As it happens, this did not in any way diminish its status as a major Romantic lyric. On the contrary, the Romantics favored fragments, whether they were formed unintentionally or intentionally, as is testified early on by the acclaim that welcomed James McPherson's *Fragments of Ancient Poetry* (1761) with its blurry image of a lost heroic world. Percy Bysshe Shelley's 'The Triumph of Life' (1822) is one of his most piercing poems; yet it is the one that he left incomplete before he drowned in the Bay of Lerici in Italy. One of the long poems we most revere of William Wordsworth's, *The Prelude* (1850), was supposed to be the introduction to a yet longer work, *The Recluse*; and so even *The Prelude* can, at a stretch, be regarded as a vast fragment, surely the largest we have in English literature.

On the continent, the Jena Romantics cultivated the writing of fragments. Friedrich Schlegel (1771–1829), who coined the word *Romantisch*, 'Romantic', as we use it today, wrote thousands of them. Some appeared in the journal *Lyceum der Schöne Künste* in 1797. Others were published in the *Athenäum*, the irruptive journal he founded with his brother, August Schlegel, and which ran for six issues from 1798 to 1800. Friedrich von Hardenberg (1772–1801), better known as Novalis, also wrote a remarkable series of fragments, the most familiar of which are 'Pollen' and 'Logological Fragments'. To understand these disconcerting texts by the Jena group we need to distinguish them from the maxims that were brought to a high level of finish by the French, beginning in the previous century. Blaise Pascal (1623–62) may not have intended that his incomplete thoughts be gathered together and published as *Pensées*, but his admirers are pleased that these brilliant and sometimes anguished remarks have survived. Different in tone and temper are the maxims of François La Rochefoucauld (1613–80) whose elegant and biting *Réflexions ou sentences et maximes morales* appeared in five editions over the period from 1665 to 1678. Equally sharp are the *Maximes et pensées* penned by Sébastien Chamfort (*c.*1740–94) which appeared the year after his death. It was Chamfort's work that attracted Friedrich Schlegel's attention, although the German was not interested in retaining the Frenchman's wit or his exquisite sense of formal balance. For Chamfort, the maxim was a highly polished gem; it had been cut from a whole stone, and its sharp lines and glittering surfaces reflected the personality of its author. In Schlegel's hands, however, the maxim was transformed into a fragment: little attempt was made, for the most part, to give a sense of formal completion to the little paragraphs or isolated sentences that he wrote. Nor was Schlegel's interest primarily in manners and morals. His concerns were wider and more philosophical, in the strict sense of the word.

Friedrich Schlegel observed that it is as deadly for the mind to form a system as for it to have no system at all, and that therefore it will have to combine both. Several things follow from this, and they tell us quite a bit about the Jena Romantics' understanding of the fragment. First of all, we should not regard the Romantic fragment as being opposed to a system but as containing the seed of an open system that might or might not be developed. If the classical fragment is merely a piece that has survived the destruction of a whole, the Romantic fragment contains a whole hidden far within itself: it promises a higher unity than is available in formal systems of philosophy like those of Kant and Hegel, for instance. So it is no surprise that in reading the *Athenäum* we come across several fragments that are almost aphorisms. Second, the incompleteness of fragments does not offer the reader a full and satisfying solution to a problem. If anything, fragments encourage the reader to think about a matter, to imagine diverse ways of engaging with it. That an idea is imperfectly embodied in a fragment is a spur to begin a dialectical exploration of the idea in all its complexity. An attentive reader might encounter a unity, but it will be one that is eventually reached by exercising the imagination, not given beforehand by form. And third, insofar as a fragment is obscure, paradoxical and finite, it reminds the reader of the limits of reason and quietly points him or her to the mystery of the infinite. The Jena Romantics were far from being orthodox Christians – Friedrich Schleiermacher (1768–1834), who became the father of liberal Protestantism, is the sole exception – but they were drawn to the mystical. These tendencies can be found in Friedrich Schlegel and Novalis. Even more clearly are they marked in the correspondence between Ludwig Tieck (1773–1853) and Karl Solger (1780–1819).

So much for the fragment, as understood in its classical and romantic forms. What about its postmodern interpretation?

* * *

No sooner is that question posed than once again we wonder when postmodern times begin, if the question is well formed, and, in any case, who might reasonably be cited as an exemplary postmodernist with respect to the fragment. Walter Benjamin (1892–1940) is usually associated with modernism rather than postmodernism, and yet since his name is cited so often by advocates of the postmodern we might be led to think of him as a precursor, if not a prophet, of the movement, at least in some respects. Certainly an essay such as 'The Work of Art in the Age of Mechanical Reproduction' (1936) is highly valued by postmodernists for its insight into the dissemination of images, although the equally well-known essay 'The Task of the Translator' (1923), with its stress on a pure language beyond all natural languages, causes them some embarrassment. Benjamin's doctoral dissertation, 'The Concept of Criticism in German Romanticism' (1920), attended closely to the Jena Romantics, including their use of fragments. Yet postmodernists find themselves more drawn to *The Arcades Project*, a collection of fragments left unfinished at his death and itself one of the most significant fragments of twentieth-century social thought. Long anticipated by Benjamin's admirers, the work did not actually appear until 1982, as the fifth volume of the author's *Gesammelte Schriften*, and so it appeared in print at just the right time to appeal to a generation that already saw itself as postmodern.

Benjamin's project was to assemble all that he could find about the arcades of Paris, which he believed to illuminate the assumptions, destinations and trajectories of nineteenth-century European culture and society. The history of the nineteenth century would not

relate itself directly, he thought. Reading the major works of the
Second Empire (1852–70) or the first half of the Third Republic
(1871–1940), for instance, would conceal more than it would reveal.
Only if we sifted among the century's discarded scraps would we be
able to discover its *Urgeschichte*, its deep history; and so Benjamin
examined apparently insignificant jottings and notes, details of the
arcades that historians would overlook. Throughout, he searched for
what he called the dialectical image: a trifle that would evoke what it
was like to be a man or woman or child living in Paris back then.
A waxworks figure, a window lit by a single candle, a passage from a
forgotten serial novel: these fragments could suddenly bring an
entire lost world back to life, if only for a moment. In that instant
we could glimpse the hopes and the sufferings, the worries and
pleasures, of people long dead.

As early as his essay on translation, Benjamin had speculated that
the original and the translation are fragments of a larger whole.
Doubtless the image is of the pure language beyond all natural languages. Chances are that Benjamin came to this image with a mystical thought in mind. His early work in particular is saturated in
Jewish spirituality, an enthusiasm he shared with his friend
Gershom Scholem (1897–1982) who became an eminent scholar
of kabbalah at the Hebrew University of Jerusalem. So perhaps the
image of fragments alludes to 'the breaking of the vessels', an important image of creation in the kabbalistic writings of Isaac Luria
(1534–72). These vessels of light contained a more radiant light, but
several of the lower ones, including primal man, broke under the
sudden pressure of the radiance, fragmented, and became the evil
that plagues the universe. What creation was to have been was
cancelled or, rather, pushed down in the scheme of things by the
blow. In other words, creation and catastrophe became the one
event. Some of the radiance was able to return to its source, but the
rest clung to the broken vessels. Our task is to discover those sparks
of pure light and restore them to the Godhead. In so doing we will be
redeemed. Could it be that Benjamin thinks there is a redemptive
aspect of translation? Or is the allusion to the breaking of the vessels
no more than a cultural gesture, made only so it might be dismissed
in the interests of enlightened, critical thought? Scholars are divided
on the matter.

In some ways Benjamin's understanding of the fragment is more
Romantic than postmodern. Those scraps of ephemera seem to contain within themselves the entire world of the nineteenth century,

the soul of early capitalism; and that idea makes some postmodernists uncomfortable. The fragment, these days, is supposed to have been freed from its task of revealing the immense in the minute. And yet the idea of regarding an entire century in terms of scraps and jottings, of presenting a complex history in terms of a montage instead of a linear narrative, appeals strongly to many postmodernists. They read Benjamin with admiration and skepticism, with pleasure and unease. For every few readers who find Benjamin's interest in the fragment tainted with mysticism, there is likely to be a reader who sees there a way towards the post-secular. And for every reader who is worried by Benjamin's materialism, there are likely to be several who find there a way in which Marxism can be rehabilitated in a postmodern mode.

* * *

In order to avoid confusion, it is best for us to adopt a distinction drawn by Maurice Blanchot. Let us call what the Jena Romantics wrote 'fragments' and what he commends to us (and what postmodernists affirm) 'the fragmentary'. For Blanchot, the Romantic conception of the fragment opens the way for us to think and write the fragmentary; and a crucial figure met on that path is none other than Friedrich Nietzsche who, as we have seen, developed a plural and dispersed way of writing. Remember his theory of perspectivalism that we pondered in the second chapter? All that material can also be understood as a consequence of thinking through to the end the notion of a fragment.

Historically important though it was, Blanchot thinks, the Romantic fragment had to be criticized from several directions before it could open onto the fragmentary. First, it posits a hidden center in each text. Second, it is considered as a self-enclosed item without due regard to the spacing between itself and other fragments. Third, it was required to be relatively short. And fourth, it remains in fee to identity: not a formal unity, to be sure, but a supposedly higher, imaginative wholeness. The fragmentary, by contrast, has no hidden center around which it revolves, for each fragment exists only in relation with others. It respects and solicits the interval, the interruption, even the silence that separates one fragment from another. A fragmentary text can be of any length – Montaigne's essays might fit the bill, for example – and it has no connection to a past or future unity; indeed, it opens up relations of an entirely new kind, precisely because the fragmentary is unable to be resolved into a unity. And finally, as a consequence of the previous point, the fragmentary is very far removed from the religious and the mystical which always, for Blanchot, answer to a transcendent unity. As we will see a little later, though, Blanchot does not wish to eliminate the infinite from the thought of the fragmentary. It remains an important feature of his ethics.

Blanchot discerned the fragmentary at work before the *Athenäum* appeared, in the diary of Joseph Joubert (1754–1824), who remains closer to us, he thought, than his contemporaries such as Diderot and Voltaire. And we might also find it in some of the writings of the Danish philosopher Søren Kierkegaard (1813–55) as well as several collections by Nietzsche. Where, though, do we locate the fragmentary today? Perhaps the most popular works composed in this way are by Roland Barthes (1915–80), whose later writings, especially *The Pleasure of the Text* (1973), *Roland Barthes by Roland Barthes* (1975) and *A Lover's Discourse* (1977) are plainly influenced by the theory of the fragmentary that Blanchot was elaborating in the 1960s. Blanchot himself deeply admired poems by René Char such as *Feuillets d'Hypnos* (1946) that were cast as fragments (and not aphorisms, as some critics believed). Towards the end of his life he was enormously impressed with Louis-René des Forêts's *Ostinato* (1997), an autobiography formed as a mosaic without once using the first person singular; and he was an early champion of the haunting volumes of *The Book of Questions* by Edmund Jabès (1912–91). Fragmentary writing was anonymous, Blanchot thought, and was therefore more likely to have more political effect than personal writing. (That strikes me as doubtful.) He argued that articles to appear in the journal with which he was associated in the early sixties, *La Revue Internationale*, should be composed entirely in fragments. That journal was never realized, yet Blanchot himself produced several fragmentary works in his later years: *The Step Not Beyond* (1973) and *The Writing of the Disaster* (1980) are the best known, although *The Infinite Conversation* (1969) can be read as a series of longer fragments, and *Awaiting Oblivion* (1962) absorbs and intrigues us in its courageous attempt to hold the fragmentary and narrative together in the one ellipse.

One abiding and powerful enemy for Blanchot is unity. It must be said, however, that he tells us very little about it. We are warned that it overtly or covertly organizes Western philosophy from

Parmenides (b. c.515 BCE) to Edmund Husserl (1859–1938), and that even the idea of God derives from a prior concept of unity. In making the latter point Blanchot may well be thinking of the Abrahamic religions: Judaism, Islam and Christianity. Perhaps, in particular, he has in mind the change that came over the Jews in their understanding of Yahweh. In the Mosaic period the Jews were monolatrists: they worshipped Yahweh while tacitly conceding the power of other deities. Yet in the post-exilic period, led by the prophets Isaiah and Jeremiah, they passed from monolatrism to monotheism, the worship of the one God, now understood as the *only* deity. It is doubtful that the Jewish confession that the Lord is One answers to a philosophical concept of unity. Or perhaps Blanchot is recalling the discussion of the One in Plato's *Parmenides* 142 where it is argued that the One is strictly ineffable and unsayable. Without a doubt, this discourse on the One influenced the early Christian concept of the deity by way of Porphyry (c.234–305) who, in his commentary on Plato's dialogue, identified the One with God. Yet since the Christian understanding of God is of a triune deity, there is no coercive reason to believe that Christianity prizes a philosophical notion of unity over and above a notion of difference. Unity and difference are held together in the Christian doctrine of God, not at the level of metaphysics but in the mystery of the Trinity. Those who affirm the Godhead beyond the Trinity, a One that resolves the distinctions between Father, Son and Holy Spirit, have always been regarded as flirting with heresy.

Also, Blanchot is surprisingly uninterested in distinguishing competing ideas of unity in philosophy. If we go back to the start of the Western tradition, Plato and Plotinus invite comparison on this score. For Plato (420–347 BCE), the One is that which unifies the many; it is beyond being but is the ground of thought. Yet for Plotinus (205–70 CE), the One is beyond being and thought. Which of the two is Blanchot arguing against? Well, *both* he would say, as well as later ideas of unity, like Kant's transcendental unity of apperception and Hegel's notion of the system. His business is not to criticize any or all theories of unity, or to weigh in on questions such as whether there is a 'unity of science' or a 'unity of truth', but to indicate that we are in a period of radical change, one in which all theories of unity are slowly breaking down. Modern astrophysics has proposed that the universe is curved, he notes in 'Ars Nova', an essay collected in *The Infinite Conversation* (1969), and if this curve has a negative sign, as is thought likely, the unity of the universe is

called into question. It can hardly be called a *uni*verse any more.
We will have to learn to figure it as discontinuous and disunited.
Also, from quite different perspectives, Mallarmé and Nietzsche,
among others, have pointed us to ways in which writing overruns
unity. Mallarmé wrote exquisitely crafted sonnets that generate
more interpretations than any unity could ever bear. Nietzsche
wrote fragmentary texts that cannot be added up to make a
single coherent thesis. If we follow these writers and scientists, we
will not only produce new kinds of fiction and poetry but also
have an immense amount of conceptual work to do, let alone the
labor of adjusting to a new sense of reality. We will have to rethink
everything that has been referred to unity, including God and truth,
being and science, the self and the book. It is that intimidating
project of reworking our entire intellectual heritage on the basis of
the fragmentary that characterizes postmodernism at its most bold.

Or at its most foolhardy, some might say. For unity is not just one
notion among others but is required for something to be intelligible
in the first place. We might reject unity as a metaphysical essence,
whether located in God or in human consciousness, but it does not
thereby follow that we must also abandon unity as a horizon of intelligibility. Besides, it might be objected, writing in fragments provides
us with no assurance of really upsetting unity. The writer of
fragments can always hold in reserve the possibility of adding more
reflections on the topic, so that in time the work could amount to a
whole, even to a full-blown system. At the least, as Derrida once
observed to Blanchot, there is always a danger that the writer of fragments can be taken to hint that he or she knows far more than is
being committed to paper. The writer of fragments can be accused of
mastery no less than the author of a coherent and complete narrative.

Let's return to the rejection of unity as an essence. I might look at
you and, like David Hume, regard you as no more than a bundle of
affects and percepts. But even if I deny that there is any principle of
identity in you, I must at least refer my perceptions of you to a horizon of unity. Otherwise, I would not be able to assure myself that
I was seeing *you* or that I was even *myself*. Against this, Blanchot and
Lévinas would join forces, at least for the moment, in order to
protest that the relation of self and other should not be set up in
terms of perception. To figure my relation with another person by
way of experience is to reduce the other person to a modification of
my consciousness. You exist to the extent that I can form a representation of you. Blanchot and Lévinas tell us that we must think

otherwise than by way of representation, presence, or even being. Ethics demands that I relate to the other person in another way entirely: infinite responsibility.

* * *

The enemy for Lévinas has several names, 'totality' and 'neuter' being two of the most common. The Greeks have provided us with a lexicon of intelligibility, he thinks. We cannot understand one another, let alone practice philosophy, without using words like 'form' (*morphe*), 'substance' (*ousia*), 'reason' (*logos*), 'thought' (*nous*) and 'goal' (*telos*). Now it is in terms of our Greek inheritance that we have long believed that something is true if and only if it is present or presentable to consciousness. It follows that, on this model, the present moment is able to hold together two quite different elements in a relation of sameness that cancels otherness. To the extent that we live within the world of philosophy, truth is bound up with sameness and totality. Is that the only world in which we live? No, Lévinas tells us: the world of the Hebrew Bible offers a different notion of truth, one that is allied to infinity instead of totality. The Jew's relation with God turns on responding to the trace of the infinite in the other person. We cannot follow this trace directly to the Infinite, however. Not even Moses was allowed to look upon God's face. The trace of the infinite passes in the face of the other person, by which Lévinas does not mean to denote eyes, nose and mouth but rather vulnerability. The path along which we walk to God is nothing if not indirect. We draw close to him when we rise from our prayers and help the stranger, the orphan and the widow.

When Lévinas speaks of transcendence, then, he does so with the other person in mind, not God. No matter where I stand, I am always beneath the other person, for social space (unlike physical space) invariably curves upward towards the other. When the other speaks to me I am addressed from above. My right to continue to exist as I have been doing is challenged. Ethics consists, Lévinas says, in yielding my place to the other person; and this passage from being to the other is what he calls 'the good'. Quite clearly, this is not an ethics that revolves around choice, for there never has been a time when I have not been summoned to help another. Nor is it an ethics that turns on drawing up a contract with the other person, so that I am responsible for my actions but not for those of others. For

Lévinas, my obligation derives from a past that has never been present. None of us can be held accountable for mortality, yet I am charged not to kill you and I hold myself responsible for not letting you die alone. And when I hear you call me I am required to answer for your hunger even though I have never personally withheld food from you. Love, for Lévinas, is not a fusion of two people, whether romantically or otherwise. It is an incessant watchfulness, even – as he says in two striking metaphors in *Otherwise than Being* (1974) – a state of being persecuted by the other, held hostage by him or her.

So there never has been a unity of the other person and me, and there never should have been. Nor have I ever been a unified self: I have always had my selfhood divided by the imperious demands of the orphan, the stranger and the widow. Ethically understood, the pronoun 'I' means 'I am here for the other person'. Were I never called by the other, I would remain in an indifferent world, and would have continued to be an atheist. But since I am called, I respond, and in responding I become a 'me'. When turning towards the other, God comes to mind, even if I do not belong to one of the historical faiths. 'God', here, is thought philosophically, not theologically. The call never stops: I can never say 'No more; I have done enough! I've done far more than my share!' I can never measure my responsibility for the other person. Quite simply, there is no representation to which I can appeal, no yardstick I can find, that would allow me to measure what I have done and what I ought to do. The meaning of ethics abides in responsibility, not in presence. So long as I affirm responsibility in preference to presence, totality can never completely occlude infinity. Even if I merely show respect to the other person by letting him or her go before me into a room, I am minimally preventing human life from freezing over, from becoming an indifferent totality.

Without a doubt, this is an ethics of the fragmentary. But is it not utopian to give everything to the other person? Yes indeed, Lévinas concedes. To give up my place in favor of the other is utopian in the etymological sense of the Greek word: *ou* + *topos*, that is, 'no place'. And is it not pathological to regard myself as responsible for everything, even other people's lack of responsibility? Surely it is. Yet these objections, reasonable though they are, miss the point being made. Lévinas is not prescribing normative moral behavior but showing that ethics has a meaning that is not reducible to presence or representation. Ethics is infinite responsibility, he maintains, not an arrangement with others that has been forged in a present moment, whether now or in the past. Such arrangements might be convenient and they might be perfectly reasonable, but they are not responses to the good. Unless we recognize that, we will always be duped by morality.

Two other things need to be noticed about this understanding of ethics as endless responsibility. In the first place, my relation to the other is entirely asymmetrical. I can ask nothing of him or her in return. To do so, Lévinas thinks, would be to reintroduce reciprocity, and then there could be no goodness. I would never really cede my place in favor of the other, for I would always be waiting to be given something in return. Notice that it follows that *Totality and Infinity* (1961) and *Otherwise than Being* do not allow their ideas to be universalized. I might owe everything to the other, but I cannot constrain you just by an argument to accept my views as binding on you. Unlike Kant, Lévinas does not invoke a moral law that makes demands on all rational beings. One is not so much persuaded by Lévinas's arguments as converted to his way of seeing things. This is not to say that his essays and treatises are without philosophical rigor. They are impressive works of phenomenology, all the more so in that Lévinas adds new methodological ideas and rich descriptions to what Husserl, Heidegger and Merleau-Ponty contributed to the discipline. To talk of being converted to Lévinas's viewpoint is merely to indicate that his understanding of ethics turns on a unique response to a singular call.

In the second place, what Lévinas calls 'ethics' is a relation only between the other person and myself. As soon as a third party intervenes, which has always happened, questions of justice must be posed. I cannot give everything to the stranger, if there is a widow calling for my aid as well. But this is no knock-down argument against ethics as infinite responsibility. It is only an indication that we need both ethics and justice, and that we need to get them in the right relation to one another: ethics before justice. Unless ethics is reckoned as foundational, Lévinas thinks, society risks becoming totalitarian in establishing programs of distributive justice. It is essential to regard the other person as a separate being, not as a participant in a neutral social existence. In his philosophy Heidegger wanted us to pass from beings to being. Lévinas reverses that movement and invites us to follow him in passing from neutral being to particular beings, people like you and me.

* * *

I said a little while ago that Blanchot and Lévinas would moment-
arily join forces to combat the proposition that the relation between
self and other can be accommodated in terms of perception. These
two friends are sympathetic to each other's writings, and in his late
fragmentary work *The Writing of the Disaster* (1980) Blanchot is in
profound agreement with the Lévinas of *Otherwise than Being*
(1974). Yet Blanchot did not wholeheartedly concur with the
Lévinas of *Totality and Infinity* (1961), and in *The Infinite
Conversation* (1969) he proposed an intriguing revision to his
friend's account of ethics.

Blanchot agrees with Lévinas that no ethics can be based on a
contract or any sort of reciprocal behavior. I must be answerable to
the other person. And yet from the other person's viewpoint am
I not the other? Surely I am, but the challenge is to answer that question without invoking a model of reciprocity. Blanchot's answer is
that double dissymmetry, not asymmetry, provides the better model
for how the other and I are related. Intersubjective space is curved in
two directions at once – upwards towards the other person, and
upwards towards me, considered as the other of the other – and
consequently there can be no reciprocity. In this ethical space, every
bit as strange as those envisaged by those mathematicians who
explore non-Euclidean geometries, I and the other person exist in an
entirely new way of engaging with each other. To see what exactly is
at issue here we need to take a step back and contemplate how
Blanchot understands the ethical rapport between two people.

There are three ways in which I can relate to another person,
Blanchot thinks. I can maintain a dialectical connection with him or
her, in which case I eventually make that person one with me. Such is
the route taken by Hegel and those who have followed him, whether
closely like Karl Marx or at a distance like Jean-Paul Sartre. (The
bondsman achieves self-consciousness, remember, by dint of his
dialectical struggle with the lord.) Or I can seek to be one with the
other, in which case I give up my individual identity in order to be
fused immediately in a higher union with the other. Such is the route
taken by the mystics, Blanchot thinks. (Marguerite Porete ends a
poem in *The Mirror of Simple Souls*, written around the end of the
thirteenth century, by saying there is no longer an 'I' to be in a
relation with God.) Yet there is a third route available to us, although

it has been kept at arm's length throughout Western history. The other person and I can be associated without any recourse whatsoever to unity. This is what Blanchot calls the relation of the third kind. Because it is neither mediated nor immediate, he also calls it the neutral relation; and because it is thoroughly atheistic, he further calls it the human relation. It is, as he likes to say, a relation without relation.

What does it mean, this curious expression 'relation without relation'? Its syntax is traditional. St Augustine in book four of his *The Literal Meaning of Genesis* talks of God as 'Measure without measure', 'Number without number' and 'Weight without weight'. Blanchot adopts the syntax to evoke ethical rather than religious transcendence. 'Relation without relation' denotes that the other person transcends me and that I transcend him or her, and that there is no possibility of measuring the distance between us. Because I am discontinuous with the other person, the passage from me to the other, and vice versa, is without bound. Only one thing can cross that distance: speech. And when we truly hear someone else's words we acknowledge the strangeness of the infinite brushing against us. It is ordinary speech that holds us together and apart. We are not two self-identical selves that are more or less whole before entering into commerce with one another. Not at all: we have been a conversation, as Freidrich Hölderlin said in a poem translated as 'Celebration of Peace'; we exist only in conversations with one another, whether they are oral or written. I choose the verb 'exist' quite deliberately, in order to present Blanchot's dark thought that unless we maintain dialogue with others, especially with those we might regard as markedly different from ourselves, we will in time be led to kill them or be killed ourselves. The conversation is infinite in the sense that it evokes the strangeness of being human – there is no representation to which we can appeal to measure our responsibility for each other – and infinite also in the sense that it cannot be terminated. Dialogue does not have the aim of bringing the other around to my point of view, or of yielding all my particularity so that I can fit neatly into the other's gaze. Its intent is to defer murder and war indefinitely.

It is worth noting that the relation without relation is confined to humans, just as Lévinas's notion of the face appears to be more or less limited to other humans. Neither Blanchot nor Lévinas shows any continuing interest in our relations with other animals. Perhaps no speech passes between my cat and me, although plainly some communication takes place; and if the face is an image of vulnerability, can one not say that a horse, a dog or a cat has a face in Lévinas's sense of the word? The general model that Blanchot proposes is of a new way of being in relation: it is anonymous (because not regulated by a self-sufficient subject), dispersed (because there is no center), deferred (because there is no limit to responsibility). If we examine Blanchot's writings on community and friendship with care, we can see that they are not without presuppositions. His sense of community is oriented more than a little by appeals to fraternity, as Derrida noted in *Politics of Friendship* (1994). Doubtless the relation without relation can be adjusted so that it includes males and females without distinction. In the same spirit, we might wonder if it can be transformed so that it takes into account our relations with animals and the natural world. Derrida would encourage us to think so: he underlines that animals have faith in one another, and sometimes in us too. (Some postmodernists would quickly add: 'Don't forget our relations to cyborgs and beings with artificial intelligence!') In other words, could it be that the human relation is unduly restricted precisely because it is a *human* relation? The question is one that, in principle, is more characteristic of postmodern than modern times. It serves to remind us that a genuine postmodern thought must take into account the damage done to nature brought about by modern understandings of our relation to the world about us. And it perhaps alerts us to contemplate the world of cyborgs into which we are perhaps heading, whether we like it or not.

That said, let us return to the human relation as Blanchot conceives it. It is neutral, he says. And we remember that Lévinas took the neuter to be an enemy. Are they talking about the same thing? No, not at all: the neuter, as Lévinas understands it, is an elimination of singular beings in favor of an indifferent being, and he takes Blanchot to have gone far in exposing this tendency in the writings of Martin Heidegger. (He says nothing about the emergence of this tendency long before, in the writings of Duns Scotus (1265/6–1308) and Francisco Suárez (1548–1617).) When Blanchot uses the word 'neuter' or 'neutral' he has something quite different in mind. The human relation is neutral, he says, because it asserts itself without reference to value or religion, feeling or justification, pleasure or knowledge. It just *is*. Such an ascetic ideal cannot be sustained, as Blanchot fully realizes, and he tells us that we live two lives that cannot be reconciled. One life is regulated by appeals to values, and it is here that we engage in dialectic: rational discourse, morality, party politics, and working for a better world. Here solidarity and unity are to be prized, since without them no political struggle can ever hope to begin. The other life we live is illuminated by a fire that never ceases to burn: a passion for the neutral relation. It is this third relation that is always supposed in any vision of a just and generous community. For Blanchot, that community is best figured in communism, not the former Soviet Union or anywhere else but in a friendship between humans that is always beyond any realized socialist state. Like Lévinas, Blanchot is utopian. And, like Blanchot, Lévinas believes we are constrained to speak always in two languages: for the former, the dialectical and the neutral, and for the latter, justice and ethics.

* * *

Unity had been a critical object for feminists before people started to talk about a postmodern world. Yet some women have taken what they need from male philosophers and writers associated with postmodernism and put their ideas to work in new ways. Luce Irigaray (1930–) is instructive in this regard, both in what she says and how she goes about it. Her early work, most notably *This Sex Which Is Not One* (1977), elaborated a critique of a widely held and undeclared assumption, that the world is constructed and interpreted by self-grounding subject, almost always figured as male. There is no *one* perspective on the world, Irigaray sensibly argues, but before we can bring to light all the other, equally legitimate viewpoints, we need to see just how thoroughly sexual difference has been bypassed, repressed and suppressed, not only in philosophy but also in politics and psychoanalysis. The female has repeatedly been seen as a weaker version of the male, and consequently fitted into a world conceived in terms of indifference and unity. To dispute that dominant male position is also to question the hegemony of the same and the one.

Having drawn attention to how varied and how deep are the ways in which the world has been constructed by and through male eyes, Irigaray sought to identify alternate, female perspectives on the world. At issue here is not an affirmation of female experience as being more immediate, more sensual or more emotional than male experience. Instead, the task is to think back through the many layers of culture and language in order to find spaces where female subjectivity might appear or even flourish and thereby to outline the conditions of possibility for a distinctive female subject to emerge. What interests Irigaray is not making women equal to men, a task associated with Simone de Beauvoir (1908–86), and one that risks erasing what is specific to women, but letting female differences emerge and develop. For as long as we conceive woman to be the other of man, we are not thinking woman *as woman*. That will occur only when we let woman appear as other, in her own ways and with her own voices. We do that by seeking those spaces in which female subjectivity are to be found.

Inevitably, given that our history has been so thoroughly patri-archal, those spaces have been opened only when the male subject has shown no interest in them, and consequently they are regarded as marginal to Western culture. They consist of fragments of speech and silence. Even so, we can find elements of what Irigaray calls female law, which includes a respect for local foods and divinities, an embracing of the rhythm of the seasons and the years, the handing down of property from mothers to daughters. Given that women are reduced to sifting fragments when in search of female subjectivity, how can they ever find a position of strength? One must not directly oppose male logic, Irigaray says by way of reply. She proposes that women mimic that logic in a playful manner, and she once charac-terized her own work as having a fling with the philosophers. Her hope is that this repetition of techniques perfected by male thinkers and writers will be managed so as to bring out the feminine in language, that is, finally to render visible what had been consigned to invisibility. Needless to say, the construction of female subjectivity is not something that can be achieved quickly; it is still largely to come, which means that the words 'female' and 'feminine' are in the process of being transformed, and doubtless will be for as far as we can see into the future.

Once the conditions of female subjectivity have been delineated, and we can hear the voices of women, the task becomes to devise ways in which sexual difference can be thought between subjects. Such is the latest phase of Irigaray's writing. When a man says 'I' he can at best lay claim to speaking as a male subject, and to some extent he must speak from within a male subjectivity, since his 'I' is irreducibly gendered. Exactly the same is true for a woman: when she says 'I' she speaks as a female subject. No one who says 'I' is whole: we are all incomplete, and that is the condition of desire. More generally, it is our lack of wholeness that can help us imagine an ethics of sexual difference. It is a minimal requirement when I relate to a woman that I acknowledge her sexual alterity. This is not something that impedes my freedom, as Hegel and Sartre believed. On the contrary, the alterity of the other person beckons me to pass from static being to fluid becoming. I do not seek to appropriate the other, nor does the other attempt to fuse with me.

In her own way, therefore, Irigaray comes to similar conclusions to those reached by Blanchot and Lévinas. Not that she accepts all that they say. In 'The Fecundity of the Caress' (1984) Irigaray criticized Lévinas for a reductive view of woman in his ethics, while in 'Questions to Emmanuel Lévinas' (1991) she tried to open a dialogue that would explore sexual difference in an affirmative way. Clearly, Irigaray differs from Blanchot and Lévinas in choosing to stress sexual difference rather than responsibility for the other in general. It is on the basis of sexual difference, she suggests, that we can begin to grasp differences of class and color, race and religion. To think in that way presumes that these differences are either the same as that between the sexes or are at least analogous with it. This is doubtful. The ways in which I differ from a Sunni Muslim living in Iran have no concrete relation to the ways in which I differ from my daughters who live in Indiana. Perhaps a deeply felt recognition of sexual difference might make me more compassionate towards those who are not the same as me, and this would surely be a good thing. But by itself it is not of much help in analyzing what separates us.

* * *

Religion is always drawn to wholeness, Blanchot argues, yet the fragmentary points us towards a non-theological age. Jean-Luc Nancy is in broad agreement, and in *The Sense of the World* (1993) suggests that we must learn to conceive the world as an absolute fragment. The world does not depend on anything: it is absolute. The world will never be complete: it is a fragment. Existence is therefore an absolute fragment. Perhaps to take that thought into our hearts and minds, right into our flesh and bones, would be to make us truly postmodern. From that perspective, Benjamin's allusion to 'the breaking of the vessels', the fragments of holy light eventually being restored to the Godhead, appears to belong to a long-lost world in which no one can seriously believe any more.

Many postmodernists think along these lines, and in doing so they risk contradicting themselves by asserting something essential and proper in postmodernism: a disenchanted and thoroughly secular understanding of the world. Look inside the word 'postmodernism' and you will see there, tightly coiled up, a number of postmodernisms. Some of these are not hostile to the words 'religious', 'mystical', and 'spiritual'; indeed, several value the postmodern for exposing us to a post-enlightenment world. This need not involve fanaticism, fideism or fundamentalism, although they remain perils, and it can invite us to view the fragmentary world in which we live as our spiritual situation. Other times have figured their spirituality differently, to be sure, but we no longer live in a world in which Protestants declare the Pope to be the Antichrist and are accordingly declared anathema by the Catholic Church, a world in which all the other religions are seen as hopelessly misguided, if not downright dangerous. Our world is irreducibly plural. If we are Christians or Jews we have to find ways of reconciling our strongest beliefs with the competing claims of Buddhists and Hindus.

For David Tracy (1939–), a contemporary American theologian, the only spirituality that is viable for us these days is one that works from and around fragments. The age of systems, including theological systems, is well and truly over. We are not to mourn a lost whole, as cultural conservatives do; and we are not to be bullied into agreeing with some of the more extreme postmodernists when they assert that the fragmentary has freed us from religion. They betray their nostalgia for modernity. With Walter Benjamin and Simone Weil (1909–43) we have exemplary thinkers for whom the fragment is the vehicle of the infinite and the hope of redemption. With the T.S. Eliot of *Four Quartets* (1942) we have a poet who, despite what his critical essays preach, practices a poetics of incompletion and a theology of hints and guesses rather than knowledge and assurance. Thus emboldened, we can look back through history and rehabilitate certain writers whose works can now speak to us more clearly: Nicholas of Cusa (1401–64), Giordano Bruno (1548–1600) and Blaise Pascal (1623–62). If we listen attentively to them, we can hear them speak, in their different ways, of divine excess and an infinite universe. They are thinkers and writers of the fragment.

Derrida questioned Tracy after he had presented his lecture at the first 'Religion and Postmodernism' conference held at Villanova University in 1997. He wondered, in particular, if fragments could really disturb a totality, and, since we can find them throughout history, if it makes much sense to associate fragments definitively with postmodernism. Tracy replied in part by distinguishing totality and God. Interestingly, he alluded to Benjamin's interest in Jewish mysticism, and noted that the divine radiance evoked in Lurianic kabbalah does not return to a totality but to the Godhead. That broken radiance, he said, is a series of fragments. They are not returned to God with the intention of restoring a lost totality, for the deity is not a unity or a wholeness but excess.

The point is well made. And yet I think that the two men would have had a more productive exchange had they distinguished the fragment and the fragmentary, and disentangled Romantic and postmodern threads as much as possible before debating our post-modern spiritual situation. There is no doubt that the fragment is turned towards the spiritual. The challenge is to make sense of spirituality in a world characterized by the fragmentary.

further reading

Bauman, Zygmunt. *Life in Fragments: Essays in Postmodern Morality.* Oxford: Basil Blackwell, 1995.

Benjamin, Walter. *The Arcades Project,* trans. Howard Eiland and Kevin McLaughlin. Cambridge: The Belknap Press of Harvard University Press, 1999.

Blanchot, Maurice. *The Infinite Conversation,* trans. and foreword Susan Hanson. Minneapolis: University of Minnesota Press, 1993.

Lacoue-Labarthe, Philippe and Jean-Luc Nancy, *The Literary Absolute: The Theory of Literature in German Romanticism,* trans., introd. and notes Philip Bernard and Cheryl Lester. Albany: State University of New York Press, 1988.

Tracy, David. 'Fragments: The Spiritual Situation of Our Times' (followed by a discussion with Jacques Derrida), in *God, the Gift, and Postmodernism,* ed. John D. Caputo and Michael J. Scanlon. Bloomington: Indiana University Press, 1999, 170–84.

Whitford, Margaret, ed. *The Irigaray Reader.* Oxford: Basil Blackwell, 1991.

the postmodern bible

What provides the greatest resistance to postmodernism? Many people, both advocates and critics of postmodernism, would have no hesitation in nominating the Bible. Here, they point out, is a monumental work, the Book of books; it stands for totality and unity, offers a sweeping narrative from creation to apocalypse, and proclaims transcendent truth without any shame. It provides the unmistakable model for canonicity, that is, for determining which texts should be held as authoritative and which should be passed over in silence; and it marks a sharp dividing line between the sacred and the secular. Here, if anywhere, is something that challenges postmodern ways of being and that postmodernism cannot digest.

This indomitable work can be found everywhere. No writing is more deeply embedded in Western culture than the Bible, and belief in the Bible has been partly responsible for spreading that same culture throughout the world. Not only has the Bible oriented the Jewish and Christian faiths, along with all the history generated by them and between them, but also it has been the single most important reference point for literature and the visual arts. Those who maintain that postmodernism divides us from the past would have the difficult task of showing how their thought and writing breaks with the biblical world. Given the Bible's tenacious hold on our imaginations, the most that could be expected by way of an answer would be the first signs of us slipping away from that grip, moving slowly and uncertainly towards something that still cannot be named by us.

Yet there are other voices to be heard, some sympathetic to postmodernism and others not, that counter this image of the Bible as a unified whole, as a grand narrative, and as a sign of radical transcendence. None of them questions that the Bible is the authoritative model of a canon, although it might be observed that the issue of canon formation is more complicated than some postmodernists suggest. Is it possible to avoid canons? I doubt it. They appear in the secular world as surely as in the sacred, among reformers and revolutionaries as well as among cultural conservatives. Some postmodernists believe – mistakenly, I think – that deconstruction overturns all canons. Certainly Derrida often attends to elements that have been pushed to the margins of a text, and sometimes he looks closely at non-canonical texts when discussing a problem. At all times, however, he affirms the richness and continuing relevance of Plato and Aristotle, Kant and Hegel, Husserl and Heidegger. It is these thinkers, he says, who point us more surely to new ways of thinking than those who believe themselves to have left the tradition but who in fact have trammeled themselves more firmly in it. Derrida does not ask us to jettison canons. He proposes that we keep alive questions of how canons are formed when reading canonical works.

There never is just the one canon, whether of Western philosophy or literature. There are always several canons in play. Most professors of English do not doubt that John Dryden and Gerard Manley Hopkins are canonical figures. Yet there are few undergraduate curricula these days that feature either poet, mostly because they occur at the cusps of literary periods. They belong firmly to the canon of Western writers though not at all securely to the current teaching canon. Professors of European philosophy treat Schelling and Hegel, Nietzsche and Heidegger, as canonical figures. Yet some professors of analytic philosophy dispute whether these are philosophers at all. They are more like murky poets than critical thinkers, they say, and hold up the natural sciences as the model for good philosophy. The canon of Western philosophy is held in common only up to the last writings of Kant.

Also, there are canons that appear and canons that fade away from lack of interest. Over the past couple of decades we have seen the emergence of a canon of post-structuralists. Could anyone seriously write a book on the subject without devoting a substantial amount of space to Derrida and Lacan, Foucault and Deleuze? To answer no is to acknowledge the pressure of a canon that is being formed. Doubtless there are rival canons. Feminists will argue for

the inclusion of Hélène Cixous, Luce Irigaray, Michèle Le Doeuff,
Sarah Kofman and Julia Kristeva. Advocates of contemporary
European Philosophy will shy away from annexing analytic philosophers such as W.V.O. Quine and Donald Davidson, Richard Rorty
and Wilfred Sellars. And it is easy to imagine a religious group
making a case for adding Michel de Certeau, Louis-Marie Chauvet,
Jean-Louis Chrétien and Hans Urs von Balthasar.

Over the same period, needless to say, there have been attempts
to form canons of postmodernists. Whom do we include? It will
partly depend on who is drawing up the list and from which institu-
tional or political ground they speak. One group might point to
Baudrillard and Lyotard, John Barth and Roland Barthes, among
others, and find reasons to pass over Blanchot and Edmond Jabès.
Another might feature Lacan and Slavoj Žižek, among others, while
not mentioning Kathy Acker and Joyce Carol Oates. We need to
remember that contemporary canons are mostly drawn up in
Europe and the United States, with the consequence that writers
from Africa and Asia, Australia and New Zealand, are often omitted
for no better reason than cultural myopia. Putting the issue of canon
formation to one side, let us try to hear what these other voices have
to tell us about the Bible's presumed unity, its status as a grand
narrative, and its affirmation of transcendence.

To be sure, people will say, the Bible is commonly taken to be a
coherent whole. The word comes from the feminine singular Latin
noun *biblia*, meaning book. Yet if we look past that meaning, we can
see that in old Latin the word *biblia* was a neuter plural form so that
it signified 'the books'. It is that older form that matches the Greek
ta biblia, the books. So there is no one book called the Bible, there
are many individual scriptures that have been gathered to form a
collection. Or, rather, *two* collections, for the Bible of the Jews, the
Tanakh, is certainly not the same as the Bible of the Christians. The
Christian Bible includes the New Testament and slightly reorders
the Hebrew Bible while recasting it as the 'Old Testament' (and
thereby making it into the longest preface in the history of Western
writing). Once this difference is acknowledged, we must notice that
there is no such thing as *the* Christian Bible. Catholics include some
scriptures, the Apocrypha, that Protestants reject; and there are a
burgeoning number of competing translations of scripture, in
English of course, and in more languages than anyone can readily
list. The Bible is indeed the Book of books, and this description
holds both unity and plurality in tension.

The view that the Bible presents a grand narrative can also be questioned. For ease of discussion, let's confine ourselves to the Christian Bible or, as I will simply say from now on, the Bible. If you read the Bible a chapter a day for however many months it takes to pass from Genesis 1 to Revelation 22, you will pass from the creation of the heavens and the earth to the last judgment and the end of time. You will encounter the history of the patriarchs, the exodus of the children of Israel from Egypt, the history of Israel under judges and kings, the prophets who proclaimed that the Messiah would come, and along the way come across a wealth of poetry and wisdom literature. Then you will hear testimonies that Jesus of Nazareth is that Messiah, read an account of what the apostles did after Jesus' resurrection and ascension, consider letters concerning the early Church, and ponder a vision that delineates the dividing of those who believe and those who disbelieve at the end of time. This is an extraordinary story, and all manner of people have thrilled to it for generation after generation.

Notice that this powerful account of our experiences of God and of God's experiences of us is quite different from what Jean-François Lyotard has in mind when he talks about sciences that employ grand narratives. These are distinctively modern discourses that seek to legitimate themselves by appealing to fables that purport to explain everything and that promise progress. Enlightenment discourses tell us that the world is rational, and determine a particular sense of 'reason' that accords with the secular sciences. They legitimate themselves by telling us that rational beings will eventually achieve universal peace and prosperity. Marxism offers a critique of Capital, and justifies itself by the story that revolutionary beings will be rewarded by having their offspring live in a future state where all will be equal. And Capitalism proposes a theory of the free market. It legitimates itself by relating that economic beings will achieve security and wealth by spending or investing their money. All these are what Lyotard calls grand narratives, and each one of them is an attempt to justify a modern discourse.

Unlike these fables, the Bible does not seek to legitimate a science or attempt to legitimate itself. Nothing could be further from the spirit of the Bible than the word 'progress'. There is hope for the Messiah in the Hebrew Scriptures and then, in the New Testament, there is hope for the Kingdom, but these are events that only God can bring about. That we should have faith that God will keep his promises is affirmed time and again in both Testaments. That we created beings can improve our lot by ourselves is repeatedly shown to be vanity, and a dangerous vanity at that. In the first centuries of the Common Era, the view is crystallized in the theology proposed by an English layman. His name: Pelagius (*fl.* 405–18). Although he did not deny divine grace, he minimized our need for it by reducing the effects of original sin on the human will. The position associated with him comes to be known as Pelagianism, and while St Augustine (354–430) wrote cordially to Pelagius in 413, he did not cease in his old age to combat Pelagianism as a virulent heresy.

Also unlike those modern narratives, the Bible does not even have a science to legitimate: the scriptures contain diverse theologies. Nor is it even the one story. There are several paths through the Hebrew Bible, and not all of them converge in the New Testament. The appearance of a unified plot that stretches from creation to apocalypse was constructed in patristic times. We see the outlines of the New Testament canon clearly for the first time in Athenasius's thirty-ninth festal letter (367), a list that was confirmed by the Council of Rome in 382 and endorsed at later synods in the late fourth and early fifth centuries. It was many centuries later when Martin Luther raised the question of the authority of some scriptures. Erasmus, a Catholic, was also troubled. As late as the Council of Trent (1546) we find the list of the canonical books being dogmatically asserted, largely as a way of containing doubts about some of them raised during the Reformation. Scripture is inspired, the Fathers at Trent declared, by which they meant that, for all the many hands that wrote it over the centuries, the true author of the forty-five books of the Old Testament and the twenty-seven of the New Testament is none other than God.

Nothing I have said implies that there are no grand narratives in Christianity. On the contrary, there are many of them, and they operate strongly on our reading of scripture. There is the Catholic narrative that tells us that Jesus designated Peter to be head of the Church and that his successors, the popes, derive their authority from this apostolic line. There is the Protestant narrative that tells us that authority derives only from faith in Christ, without the mediation of the Church. Its grand narrative turns on the Kingdom rather than the Church. There is what people call the Thomist narrative: faith and reason, when held in the right balance, will lead us to the truth. And there is the Calvinist narrative that the Reformation did not mark a new beginning but returned us to the pure origin of

the faith. The grand narratives in Christianity are ecclesial and theological. They appeal to scripture but do not simply arise from it. To
show incredulity towards those grand narratives, which Lyotard
believes to be symptomatic of the postmodern, would be to express
skepticism at ecclesial claims for legitimation and theological
quests for a complete and coherent system. We always need to keep
in mind that the faithful regularly appeal to the Bible when criticizing aspects of the Enlightenment, Marxist and Capitalist narratives.
And we should not forget also that ordinary Christians cite the
Bible when distancing ourselves from various decisions of church
authorities and when debating reductive positions commended by
theologians.

Finally, what can be said of the biblical teaching of transcendence? Is there a more subtle understanding of what the Bible proclaims than what postmodernists usually offer? The first thing to say
is that while the scriptures bear witness to transcendence they do so
in a variety of ways, all of them partial and all of them inadequate to
what they affirm. There have been attempts to gather these witnesses
together and arrange them into a unity. Even with the founding
documents of the New Testament, however, the result has not been a
success. In the late second century Tatian attempted to recast the
four gospels as a continuous narrative in his *Diatessaron*, but his
example has never seriously been followed. More rewarding as spiritual reading is the *Catena Aurea* of St Thomas Aquinas: a gathering
of passages about the four gospels by the Church Fathers, put
together so that a continuous commentary is produced, one that
implies the unity of Church teaching. In general, though,
modern and postmodern biblical critics concur in pointing out
differences between the gospels. What once failed with regard to the
gospels in the *Diatessaron* has no chance of succeeding with the
Bible as a whole.

If you begin reading the Bible looking for transcendence, you will
quickly find obstacles placed in your path by the text itself. No
sooner have you reached Genesis 1:2 than you will encounter a
massive one. For the Bible tells us that God fashioned the world from
that which was 'without form and void' (*tohu vabohu*) and from a
primal ocean, 'the deep' (*tehom*). He did not create everything out of
nothing, according to this verse, and no passage later in scripture
explicitly contradicts this view. The traditional image of the God
whose transcendence is so absolute that he creates the heavens and
the earth *ex nihilo* is not biblical but theological. We find it proposed

by St Irenaeus (130–200) in his *Against Heresies* II. xxx. 9. In book twelve of his *Confessions,* St Augustine proposed ways of bringing Genesis 1:2 into line with the doctrine of creation out of nothing, and more recently the major Reformed theologian Karl Barth (1886–1968) confessed in *Church Dogmatics* III. i that Genesis 1:2 is one of the most difficult verses in the Bible to interpret. In his judgment the verse speaks neither of something that preceded creation nor of something that God posited and then worked over during creation. Rather, the verse indicates, by way of a borrowing from myth, the world that was firmly rejected by God in the act of creation.

As you continue reading through the Hebrew Scriptures, it becomes increasingly hard to affirm that the Bible offers a unified, metaphysical idea of a transcendent deity. The God who visits Adam in the cool of the evening, the God who stalks Moses with intent to kill him, and the frightening God of Hosea differ markedly from the impassable God of the philosophers. The God who is disclosed in the Shekinah, the dwelling of the divine in the Tabernacle after the destruction of the Temple in 587 BCE, and the God who is revealed in the acts and preaching of Jesus never converge on an icy being of timeless transcendence. Biblical men and women knew that God was intensely involved in their world. Of course, they believed that God transcends all creation, but what that actually meant changed over time.

In a preliminary way, then, we have reason to think that the common postmodern image of the Bible as a unity, a grand narrative, and an affirmation of untroubled transcendence is a caricature. More than that, we have reason to think that the Bible can be approached from the same perspective that has sometimes been used to discredit it. We can consider the hypothesis that there is a 'postmodern Bible'.

* * *

When the Bible and Culture Collective put together their study *The Postmodern Bible* (1995) they took their enemy to be the higher criticism. The emphases of this venerable adversary are historical context and philology; and with the tools of the secular sciences, from heraldry to palæography, it is possible, so its practitioners believe, to sift history from legend.

Whether it was an ancestor or an antecedent, the *Tractatus Theological-politicus* (1670) must be named at the start of any discussion of the higher criticism. This incisive work, published anonymously by Baruch Spinoza (1632–77), steadily maintains that the miracles described in the Hebrew Bible were natural events that were misinterpreted by those who recorded them. The beliefs of the prophets were of their time and are not binding on those who have gained intellectual sophistication through the study of philosophy. Such ideas are germane to the higher criticism, and they were applied to the New Testament in the following two centuries. By the late nineteenth century, the historical-critical school had fragmented. Nowadays we talk of source criticism, and think in particular of Julius Wellhausen (1844–1918); we talk of redaction criticism, and look back to Wilhelm Wrede (1859–1916), as one of several practitioners. Equally, biblical scholars now learn as part of their basic training about the form criticism of Hermann Gunkel (1862–1932) and Rudolf Bultmann (1884–1976) and, more recently, about the canonical criticism exemplified in James A. Sanders's *Torah and Canon* (1972). Without these strands of biblical criticism we would have less reliable knowledge about the authorship of scripture, about the dates of composition, and the theological intent of passages and entire books.

If we take a few steps back and let all these critical programs resolve themselves into the one overarching movement, the historical-critical school, we can see that they share a common assumption. They are all cued into the Enlightenment grand narrative, and are therefore thoroughly modern in their assumptions about the world. It is science that reveals the truth, they assure us, and neutrality is the proper medium for scholarly investigation into scripture. There is no surprise, then, in learning that the higher critics give little or no credence to items that have sustained the faithful for centuries: the virgin birth, the bodily resurrection, the ascension into heaven, not to mention the miracles and theophanies. The truths that the historical-critical approach extract from scripture come at the price of treating it as a distant object, far removed from its liturgical and spiritual roles for the believer, and equally sequestered from its effects in contemporary culture. A biblical critic has to suspend his or her religious beliefs before practicing historical criticism. Or, if we look at the statement from the other side, he or she has to affirm a belief in modernity.

So we can see why the authors of *The Postmodern Bible* would wish to distinguish themselves sharply from the modernism of biblical criticism. For them, the modern Bible has become no more than a dusty item in a museum, cared for by curators whose critical assumptions are in dire need of rejuvenation. What is needed, the postmodernists argue, is to see how the Bible will respond to various new critical approaches to literature. And so they tell us about the main critical schools of the time: deconstruction, psychoanalytic criticism, rhetorical criticism, feminism and ideological criticism. Even structuralism and reader-response criticism are included, not because they are postmodern but because they have been taken up by some exegetes and the positions need to be critiqued for their benefit.

You will have noticed that all these new critical approaches are imported from the study of literature where they had constellated in the late 1970s and throughout the 1980s. And you will have suspected that there is another enemy within the sights of the Bible and Culture Collective: those literary critics of a more traditional stripe who have applied themselves to the Bible. Robert Alter and Frank Kermode's *The Literary Guide to the Bible* (1987) is soundly taken to task for excluding the various critical positions that are now asterisked for our attention. From the Collective's perspective, Alter and Kermode have protected not only the biblical canon but also the canon of literary criticism. In doing so, they are charged with failing to declare the ideological character of their act. They are naughty boys, the Collective declares, shaking their many heads as one.

It is regrettable that the Bible and Culture Collective adopted such a polemical attitude towards *The Literary Guide to the Bible*. For one thing, it suggests that there is a keen difference between the modern and the postmodern. Yet as they rightly acknowledge in their introduction, the postmodern is not a rejection of the modern; it is a series of reflections on the impossibility of modernity to complete its own projects. For another thing, the castigation of Alter and Kermode draws attention to something that makes many people uneasy when they see the word 'postmodern' linked to a name like Shakespeare or a universe like the Bible. At its best, the lens 'postmodern Bible' should bring into focus new ways of reading the texts contained in both Testaments; and consequently it will expand our understanding of the Bible. Yet there is always the danger that the reader will object that the adjective 'postmodern' is far too narrow an aperture to use with respect to the Bible. What can

be achieved by presenting a postmodern Bible when the Bible itself
is so much larger and richer than postmodernism?

That question should be kept in mind: it deters us from overvalu-
ing the present. And it should be kept to one side of the mind, for
unless it responds to contemporary concerns, the Bible will quickly
become a relic. The same objection made to our associating postmodernism and the Bible was once made (and still is, from time to
time) to bringing literature and the Bible into dialogue. The issue we
need to keep before us is how forcefully the Bible responds to the
pressure of the questions that we put to it. So let us look at how the
Bible has been used by some of our contemporaries. All of the
people I will introduce have been called postmodernists at one time
or another, although none of them thinks that it is an appropriate
designation.

* * *

Harold Bloom is mentioned just twice in *The Postmodern Bible*, and
not being assimilated by the Collective would surely please him. As a
literary critic, he finds little to help him in the writings of Derrida
and Foucault, Baudrillard and Lyotard. He is, as he likes to say, a
canonical critic, a reader whose most pressing questions turn on the
ways in which a writer veers away from the authoritative works of a
tradition in order to clear imaginative space for himself or herself.
This swerve from earlier writings is perverse and violent: a strong
writer misreads those who come before him or her. Without this
initial misreading, there can be no originality, and originality for
Bloom is the *sine qua non* of art. This quality of invention is found
only in terms of a relation with the powerful works of our tradition.
Modern poets must come to terms with their predecessors or
be silenced by them. To be a poet writing in English now is to
engage with Wallace Stevens and, behind him, William Blake and
William Wordsworth. Behind the Romantics stands Milton; and,
behind him, looms William Shakespeare. And if we go back far
enough we find ourselves confronting the prime mover of our
tradition, the Hebrew Bible.

The origin of the Western tradition, Bloom argues, is not Homer
but an author whose name will probably puzzle you. It is not
even a name but an initial: J. We owe the initial to Julius Wellhausen
who, drawing on the work of older contemporaries, ventured the

hypothesis that the first five books of the Bible, the Pentateuch, is a composite work put together from four documents. There is material written by the Elohist (E), deriving from the eighth century BCE and by the Deuteronomist (D), who wrote in the following century, by the much later Priestly writer (P), who was active in the fifth century BCE, and by the Jahwist (J), the oldest of them all, who composed his stories in the ninth century before the Common Era. This documentary theory, as it is called, was an important contribution to the higher criticism, and its roots in modernity are everywhere apparent.

Unlike Wellhausen, Bloom claims J as an author, not a hypothesis. In the stories of Jahweh forming Eve from Adam's rib, Cain's murder of Abel, Noah and the Ark, Abram's departure from Ur, Jacob's wrestling with the angel, Moses' colloquy with Jahweh on Mount Sinai, and so many others, we have a writer of immense imaginative power. Stories of that caliber are not written by a hypothesis but by an individual, Bloom stoutly maintains. And if we look closely at those stories, without wearing the blinkers of either belief or disbelief, we can recognize that they are narratives of supreme irony. Their literary structure consists of incommensurable realities colliding with one another: the mortal Jacob wrestling with an angel, the man Moses talking with his creator, and so on. Our difficulty in reading these stories is that we know them, or *think* we know them, far too well. After all, so much of our tradition has elaborated itself by reference to them. That tradition has tended to take J too much at her word – yes, Bloom ventures that the author is female, a member of the court of King Rehoboam of Judah – and both Judaism and Christianity at their most normative (that is, orthodox) are guilty of failing to read metaphors as metaphors. Unable to assimilate J's originality, we defend ourselves from her ironic vision of human and divine relations by regarding her stories as mere anthropomorphic images of God.

Notice that in his understanding of the Western literary tradition, Bloom refuses to distinguish secular from sacred writing. That division makes no sense, he says. You cannot place the Bible here, and Shakespeare there, saying that the former is sacred and the latter is secular. They are both instances of highly imaginative writing to which our tradition answers in complicated ways, and there is a profound unity of the imagination. You can, if you are of a post-enlightenment temperament, say that the Bible and Shakespeare are both secular. Or, if you are otherwise committed, you can say that both are sacred. What you cannot do and remain coherent is distribute that distinction across the field of imaginative writing.

Three things are tied up here, and we need to disentangle them if we are to have any understanding of Bloom's sense of the Bible. In the first place, Bloom is sublimely uninterested in arguing for a canon at the level of theory. A pragmatist, he is less interested in whether something is true than in whether it works. Rejecting the distinction between sacred and secular works if it gets the desired result, and for Bloom that result is recognizing the contingency and force of a tradition of imaginative writing that begins with J and that stretches across the millennia to encompass us. Second, the imagination is a metaphor for what is original and irreducible in the self. We can call this a subjective appropriation of the truth, as long as we do not take 'truth' in any metaphysical sense. I am individualized by my imagination, that is, by my subjective engagement with art. In other words, Bloom is a Romantic. Third, the imagination offers the only redemption that is available to me. I can call it 'sacred' or 'secular' but in the end it does not matter. I am put in contact with the imagination not by having faith in culture but by reading the texts around me in such a way that I discover my deep self, the 'I' that precedes the self that others see when they encounter me. And so Bloom is a latter-day Gnostic, one with a pronounced taste for kabbalah. We will not be saved by following the Law or by believing in Jesus. We will be saved only if we become ourselves, if we finally recognize in ourselves that which has not been fashioned by culture and society. Such a salvation is wholly immanent, needless to say, but it results in a *gnosis*, a knowing, that prevents us from being the dupes of culture and society.

Surely Bloom is not a postmodernist, it will be objected (not least of all by him), and with very good reason. He affirms a deep 'I' whereas postmodernists maintain that the human subject has no substance whatsoever. He asserts that there is a canon of literary works, and postmodernists commonly reject canons as élitist, preferring instead to talk of an archive from which they can draw as they see fit. And he conceives artworks not as texts but as relationships of psychic force. That he has learned from Freud and Nietzsche is plain, although it is not the Freud and Nietzsche primarily valued by Lacan and Derrida. Far from being a postmodernist, then, we might say that Bloom is antithetical to them, and they to him. Before leaving the matter at that, though, it is worthwhile to reflect for a moment or two. In the second chapter we agreed that the three main marks of postmodernism were anti-essentialism, anti-realism, and anti-foundationalism. How does Bloom stand with respect to these?

A pragmatist, Bloom is therefore an anti-essentialist. All talk of presence is delusive, he thinks, a consequence of people's faith and nothing more. Our language does not describe the world 'out there' in a clear and coherent manner, he tells us; rather, it indicates, in a highly coded manner, what occurs far within the self. He is an anti-realist, then, although of an unusual kind, with only a thorough-going subjectivist like Kierkegaard for company. And at no time does Bloom affirm that there are solid grounds. All imaginative writing is based on prior imaginative writing, right back to the primal author, J, whose narratives are substitutions for losses we can hardly begin to conceive. Now if Bloom is anti-essentialist, anti-realist and anti-foundationalist, he is kin to postmodernists, even if neither he nor they recognize the family resemblance. That he has no taste for the vocabulary or many of the prized texts of postmodernism is readily conceded, and that he poses difficulties for card-carrying postmodernists at every turn is also admitted. What Bloom does not share is the postmodernists' attitude towards the world about him. He has 'attitude' of another kind entirely.

* * *

Bloom and Blanchot are as distant from one another as any two literary critics could be. Bloom argues that the strong writer swerves from earlier works, and in doing so discovers and affirms his or her 'I'. The writers who interest Blanchot, however, swerve from the possible to the impossible, from power and selfhood to the menacing outside, the space of endless dying. In writing, Blanchot thinks, you lose your 'I'. Bloom asserts the value of aesthetics, while Blanchot argues that the aesthetic is precisely that which blocks a proper vision of literature. It will therefore not be unexpected to hear that Blanchot develops a quite different account of the Bible from the one we have just considered.

In 'The Absence of the Book', the final chapter of *The Infinite Conversation* (1969), Blanchot proposes that the Bible is the prototype of all books, sacred or secular. Above all, the Bible speaks of unity, Blanchot thinks. It tells us of the One God, and the Ten Commandments contain within themselves the One Law, which Blanchot takes to be the Law of Unity. To the extent that anything, even a passionate work of atheism, is a *book* it remains theological because it contains a covert reference to the Bible as the Book of books. Only if we begin to think of the third relation, the relation without relation, in which we maintain ourselves in a dispersed and deferred way of being, can we drift away from the world as it has been determined by the Bible. Ironically, it is the Bible that gives us a seed that, when suitably tended, blossoms into that new way of being. For the Bible is a work of testimony; it tells us of a covenant formed between God and human beings. What ties humans and God together is none other than speech. If we could only detach that testimony from the Bible, remove it from the book, we could divest it of all traces of a sacred aura and put it to work as ethics. And that, Blanchot thinks, is exactly what has been slowly happening for centuries and is now emerging with a particular force.

What we owe to Israel, Blanchot thinks, is not the revelation of the One God but the revelation of speech. Clearly, there can be no relation between an infinite deity and a finite created being: no dialectic can keep the two in tandem, and mystical union dissolves all relation. Yet the Hebrew Bible shows us how men, women and children can hold ourselves in relation with the infinite God by way of prayer. Only prayer allows us to engage in a relationship of familiarity with the unknowable deity, only prayer allows God to talk with us and we to talk with him. What needs to be done, Blanchot suggests, is to translate the divine relation into the human relation. Instead of perpetuating a relationship with the divine Other through prayer, we should recognize that the human relation of self and other, other and the other's other, is maintained through speech. Since there is no way of measuring my responsibility for the other person, he or she is infinitely distant from me, like the God of the Jews. My sole way of maintaining a rapport with that person is speech. Not to communicate will eventually have a dire consequence, as we saw in the last chapter. Our choice is brutally simple: speak or kill.

Speech is therefore the medium of ethics, for Blanchot. Notice that he does not take 'speech' in the narrow sense of voice. Not at all: he affirms a notion of plural speech, which, as he explains, is to be understood as the speech of writing. Partly he derives this view from the kabbalistic writings of Rabbi Isaac the Blind, the thirteenth-century Jewish scholar, and partly from the early essays of Jacques Derrida. In *Writing and Difference* (1967) and *Of Grammatology* (1967) Derrida argues that speech and writing are both conditioned by a movement of difference and deferral that he calls *la différance*. From Isaac the Blind Blanchot draws the idea of a mystical Torah. The Jews believe that God gave Moses the Law, or Torah, in two forms: oral and written. The letters inscribed on the scrolls are to be supplemented by the oral teachings. Now the Jerusalem Talmud, the vast commentary on the Mishnah, the first written summary of the oral Law, tells us that Torah existed before creation. Its letters were black fire that flared against a background of white fire. Now Isaac the Blind ventures the idea that the true written Torah is to be found in the white fire. On this mystical interpretation, the Bible preserves oral Torah while written Torah cannot be read. Only Moses could contemplate this primal text, and only the great prophets could gain any insight into it, however limited. Mystical Torah is therefore first writing. It has no origin, and it transgresses all laws, even the Law that Moses carried down from Mount Sinai. And so mystical Torah compromises the unity of Torah even before it is given to the children of Israel.

Blanchot admires Jewish mysticism because, unlike its Christian counterpart, it does not presume the possibility of fusion with God. Yet we should not take him to be defending mysticism in any sense. His focus is ethics, and it is Lévinas's later writings, especially *Otherwise than Being or Beyond Essence* (1974), that provide him with the best possible account of ethics as infinite responsibility. Indeed, it is Lévinas who states that all true discourse is discourse with God, by which he means that we are always in an asymmetric relation with another human being. This transcendence is, as we have seen, ethical, not religious, and Lévinas strongly implies that both Judaism and Christianity derive their sense of religious transcendence from a prior but unacknowledged sense of ethical transcendence. No one today can believe in biblical cosmology, he says, yet we can all learn from the Bible, if we read it with due care. When we do so, he thinks, we learn 'Thou shalt not kill' (Exod. 20:13) is not solely an injunction against murder but, more important, it is a command to be aware of the many ways in which we are indirectly responsible for letting men, women and children die from poverty and oppression, ways which allow us to retain good consciences because we have not lifted a hand against them. (Notice that Lévinas says nothing about non-human animals. His ethics is limited to the sphere of the human.) We should remember Samuel's response to the Lord's call, 'Here am I' (1 Sam. 3:4). This is the right response to any call from any person. To read the Bible properly is to realize that the land flowing with milk and honey is not for us to take but is to be given to the other. One can only wonder what would have happened had Moses come up with that interpretation of God's promise.

So the Bible, for Lévinas, is a source of wisdom that is at heart different from the philosophy devised by the Greeks. It is not a body of scriptures of interest only to a particular people. On the contrary, it offers a wisdom that can inform all folk. Or, turning the thought around, being Jewish is the way of being human that is shared by all men and women, boys and girls. All of Western thought has been developed from those two bases, and to some extent they remain distinguishable. Although Greek philosophy has provided us with a vocabulary that renders the world intelligible, it has not yet managed to translate all of biblical wisdom into its terms. Not everything has been recast in terms of the metaphysics of presence, and it is the Hebrew Bible that provides resistance to that inexorable movement. In doing so, it keeps open the exigency of ethics.

* * *

Towards the end of *The Writing of the Disaster* (1980) Blanchot tells the story of the Messiah being discovered at the gates of Rome, sitting among beggars and lepers. Someone recognizes him, and asks him when he will come. To which the Messiah answers that he will come today if his voice will be heard.

This little tale distinguishes ordinary time from messianic time, and indicates that the two never coincide. That the Messiah is here, right now, does not mean that he has come. By the same token, we do not wait for the Messiah to reveal himself in a future present: the responsibilities to which we are called by belief in the Messiah press upon us now, as they have always done. We must always call 'Come' to the Messiah, even if he is here among us, because there is a division between the order of history and the order of faith or, if you prefer, between the order of law and the order of justice. Such, at least, is what Derrida has learned from Blanchot's story.

I relate all this by way of introducing Derrida's reflections on the Bible. In the first chapter, one of your guides told you a little about the philosopher's reading of Genesis 11:1–9, the story of the Tower of Babel. Derrida has also written about Genesis 22:1–14, the *Akedah*, or binding of Isaac by Abraham, and in the same work,

The Gift of Death (1992), has meditated on the fifth and sixth chapters of Matthew. Also, Derrida has written on several verses taken from the Revelation of St John the Divine, especially the final chapter. The passage begins with John writing, 'And the Spirit and the bride say, Come. And let him that heareth say, Come. And let him that is athirst come. And whosoever will, let him take the water of life freely' (Rev. 22:17). And it ends with John offering a benediction, and, immediately beforehand, saying, 'He which testifieth these things saith, Surely I come quickly. Amen. Even so, come, Lord Jesus' (Rev. 22:20). It is the word 'come' that calls for analysis, Derrida thinks, and in elaborating his commentary on it he remembers what Blanchot said about the coming of the Messiah.

The first thing to say about Derrida's biblical interpretations is that they are always partly framed by philosophical concerns or, more accurately, by concerns that exceed the economy of philosophy. When reading the story of Babel, Derrida keeps one eye firmly on Walter Benjamin's essay on translation, 'The Task of the Translator', and allows the biblical story to lead him to a more radical understanding of translation than Benjamin offers. When pondering the terrifying tale of Abraham binding his son Isaac, Derrida remains close to Kierkegaard's reading of the story in *Fear and Trembling* (1843), a text that also broods over his exegesis of Matthew. And finally, when reading the book of Revelation, Derrida keeps an essay of Kant's in mind, 'On a Newly Arisen Superior Tone in Philosophy' (1796). In principle any text, Derrida says elsewhere, can be used to help read any other text. Here, though, there are clear connections between the biblical and non-biblical writings.

We also need to remember that Derrida's biblical interpretations are not exegeses. He does not read scripture with a view to doing theology or even philosophical theology. His concern here, as with literature, is to invent something quite new, at the risk that it might turn out to be monstrous. Indeed, this is the very thing that interests him in the word 'Come' in Blanchot's story of the Messiah, in *The Writing of the Disaster*, and in the book of Revelation. To say 'come' is not to call something or someone into your presence whose identity has been fully determined in advance. On the contrary, Derrida says, it calls the event itself with all its unforeseen dimensions and possible complications. The etymological relation between 'come' and 'event' is more evident in French than in English: *viens* and *événement* belong to the same family as *venir*, the verb 'to come'. To these words we can add others that Derrida involves in his discussion: *avènement* (advent), *avenir* (future), *aventure* (adventure) and of course *inventer* (to invent).

There is no such thing as an event that we can fully know in advance, Derrida points out. Any event contains, as a structural feature, the possibility that it can fall short of our expectations, exceed them, or surprise us in some way. Of course that possibility might not be realized with a particular event. I can throw a ball up in the air while looking straight ahead, intend to catch it in my open hand, and often enough I do just that. The event is unremarkable. Yet at times the possibility of the event misfiring is realized. I can throw a ball up into the air and then miss it when it falls down. Or I can throw it up and, strange to believe, it stuns a magpie flying low that then suddenly falls onto my head. In Derrida's terms, no event has an uninterrupted horizon of expectation. So when I call 'Come' to an event, it is always possible for the unexpected to occur.

What happens if I call 'Come' to the Messiah? I will not be calling someone whose identity is fully known to me, determined in advance of his arrival. I will not be able to calculate with any confidence what the Messiah will do, even though I will have anticipations, expectations and prejudgments. The Just One will not fit neatly into the categories and laws of the present time: that much I know because law and justice never entirely coincide. If the Just One comes, I will not at first be able to identify him positively, for he will exceed whatever norms have been put in place by a society or by a religious group. To use Derrida's terms once again, the Messiah will not appear under the sign of the possible, what I know and am familiar with, but under the sign of the impossible, what will surprise me, challenge me, upset me, perhaps even distress me.

To say 'Come', Derrida tells us, is to announce an apocalypse. For it will be a disaster if the Messiah arrives and I find myself at odds with him, disappointed by him, or changed in a totally unforeseen way by him. This is not an apocalypse that will mark the end of the world but, as Derrida says with a glance towards his friend Blanchot, an apocalypse without apocalypse. The general structure of 'come' is to bring forth what can disturb by its very otherness. I can call my wife from work and say, 'Get a babysitter, and come to dinner at the La Salle Grill tonight', having in mind a quiet romantic evening. But she might arrive and, over dessert, tell me that she no longer loves me.

Derrida's commentary on some verses of Revelation tells us nothing that would replace a patient exegesis, and it certainly is not intended to do that. Yet it makes us attend to a crucial word in Revelation and in Christian spirituality in general. If a Christian prays 'Come' to Jesus, as we are enjoined to do, then we should be aware of what we are doing. It is important for us to mark the otherness of Jesus Christ, not to believe that we already fully know who he is. No one who reads the New Testament has the right to think that the Jesus variously represented there is altogether given to us in the order of knowledge. We pray with a deep trust that God does not deceive us, yet we need to remember that our prayer is addressed to a transcendent deity whose otherness is not to be reduced. Even the most vigilant Christian succumbs from time to time to accommodating God to a preferred image of him, and it is salutary to be reminded that when we call 'Come' we are perhaps calling a Savior who will shatter the image of him that we have so carefully constructed.

In other essays, most notably 'How to Avoid Speaking' (1989), Derrida will tell us that as soon as we address ourselves to God we are no longer making a pure prayer, that is, praying to the Other as other, for the word 'God' in Judaism or Christianity is already a bundle of scriptural images and theological determinations. If I pray to the Father, to Christ, or to the Trinity, I am making a *Christian* prayer, not offering a pure prayer. Already, I have reduced the otherness of the Other. Doubtless this is so, and the believer will respond by rejoicing that God has revealed himself to us. We are liberated from the horror of addressing ourselves to what is completely foreign to us. Yet those same scriptural and theological determinations stress that God's otherness is to be respected: his unveiling always involves a reveiling. Derrida's remarks on the book of Revelation tell us less than we are used to finding in biblical commentaries, and are not designed to serve as theological propositions. Yet for the believer they can serve another, supremely important, function. They can aid us in avoiding idolatry.

further reading

Adam, A.K.M., ed. *Postmodern Interpretations of the Bible: A Reader.* St Louis: Chalice Press, 2001.

Aichele, George, *et al. The Postmodern Bible.* New Haven: Yale University Press, 1995.

Bloom, Harold. *Ruin the Sacred Truths: Poetry and Belief from the Bible to the Present*. Cambridge: Harvard University Press, 1989.

Fenves, Peter, ed. *Raising the Tone of Philosophy: Late Essays by Immanuel Kant, Transformative Critique by Jacques Derrida*. Baltimore: The Johns Hopkins University Press, 1993.

Jobling, David, *et al.*, eds. *The Postmodern Bible Reader*. Oxford: Basil Blackwell, 2001.

Prickett, Stephen, ed. *Reading the Text: Biblical Criticism and Theory*. Oxford: Basil Blackwell, 1991.

Schwartz, Regina, ed. *The Book and the Text: The Bible and Literary Theory*. Oxford: Basil Blackwell, 1990.

postmodern religion

If you visit a good bookshop in a big city and look over the religion shelves you will find an increasingly large selection of books that use the expressions 'postmodern religion', 'postmodern Christianity', 'postmodern God' and 'postmodern theology' in their titles or sub-titles. These are perplexing words. In all likelihood a postmodern Christianity would be anti-essentialist, anti-realist and anti-foundationalist. Yet that doesn't seem to square with what most Christians think about the faith. Surely they believe that Christianity teaches that there is an essence to human beings, namely our souls. They think that language hooks up with reality, and so they are realists. And since they believe that God exists and that he created the heavens and the earth, they must hold that there is a foundation to reality, God himself. Given all that, how can there be such a thing as 'postmodern Christianity' or 'postmodern religion'?

Before answering the question, we need to put a possible confusion to one side. We need to distinguish religion, as practiced in postmodern times, from postmodern religion. Perhaps it looks like an overly fine distinction, but in fact there is a vast gulf between the two. Let's take them one at a time, beginning with religion in postmodern times. That there *is* religion today needs to be acknowledged at the outset. Those modern thinkers like Marx, Nietzsche and Freud who thought that religion would fade away in future generations were quite mistaken. To be sure, attendance in the mainstream churches in Europe has declined steadily over the last few decades. For a variety of reasons, large numbers of babyboomers

107

and their children do not find themselves spiritually nourished by what most Catholic and Protestant churches have to give them. Of course, many parents in France and Italy, countries that have been traditionally Catholic, still want their offspring to be baptized, although their reasons differ from those their grandparents had. Nowadays the motivation often tends to be more psychological and social than confessional. They want their children to be socially integrated and to imbibe morality, or they desire a ritual to mark an important event in their lives, or they vaguely believe that there is something, however obscure, that speaks to them in the liturgy.

Over and against this tepid faith, though, you find many people who have abandoned the churches of their grandparents because they find them too wishy-washy in what they stand for. The churches, they think, do not preach Christ as a contradiction to the world but merely as a mild corrective to it. And so they go in search of what will be a greater sign of contradiction. Some remain within the orbit of Christian belief, and prefer to attend Pentecostal gatherings, crusades or informal prayer meetings. Here and there you find evangelical churches swelling; and almost everywhere you find people tuning into gospel preachers on TV late at night; and you even find strict religious communities attracting novices for the first time in over a decade. In the cacophony of postmodern times, the silence of an enclosed order must seem appealing, as does the reassurance of a beautiful and ancient liturgy. Also, as has happened since the sixties, people look to Asian religions. In recent decades, Buddhism has been more successful than Christianity in teaching people about contemplation. The rich heritage of mystical prayer, beginning with the Desert Fathers, is not being taught as widely as it needs to be, and so there is the inevitable result that many people have to look outside the Church to find what once sustained the Church. Far more than in the sixties, though, people today are seeking solace or thrills in alternative religions. They are drawn to New Age communities and even Pagan rites. You find people experimenting with Wiccan ceremonies, becoming involved with cults like The Family and Heaven's Gate. Postmodernity is not only an age of the cult but also it is the age in which you learn equally about Cistercian Abbeys and Cosmic Traveling on that great leveler, the Internet.

Yet everyone knows that the religiosity that most violently asserts itself today is fundamentalist. We look uneasily at some groups and wonder exactly where the line is that divides fundamentalism from fanaticism, and how in this area we would begin to distinguish religion from politics. We are rightly frightened by Osama bin Laden and his terrorist network, Al-Qaeda, partly because of their militant interpretation of Islam. We were disturbed when we saw news clips of Afghanistan in the 1990s: in Kabul the Taliban hanged men and women found guilty of adultery and whipped spectators at football matches when they cheered their team. And we remain wary of fundamentalism in Iran and the Sudan. Exactly *what* concerns the West in those two countries is often not at all clear. Sometimes the fear is that the Islamic peoples have not passed through a period of secular enlightenment and established distinct roles for religion and government. Accordingly, there is a fear that Islamic fundamentalism is radically at odds with democracy: a view that is being eroded by recent progressive movements in Iran. And sometimes the fear is simply of that which is alien, foreign, and therefore dangerous. We are afraid of what we do not understand, and we do not understand societies that seem premodern and unwilling to embrace modernity to the extent or in the ways that we have done.

The very expression 'Islamic fundamentalism', used so often in the Western media, is an index of how poorly understood Islam is. When commentators talk about Islamic fundamentalists the impression is usually given that these are groups akin to Christian fundamentalists: people clinging to a cramped sense of scripture as literally true (in English translation, of course), narrow-minded rednecks who will not allow evolution to be taught in schools, uncritical social conservatives who despise all liberals and the education that has given them fancy ideas. No awareness is given by the media that in Islam there is no rough-and-ready distinction between fundamentalists and liberals, as there is in Christianity. Only in the United States, home of Southern Baptists and others like them, does it seem appropriate to talk of Islamic fundamentalism. Even then, with a group in the United States like the Nation of Islam and a leader like Louis Farrakhan, it is doubtful that Muslims from Iran or Pakistan would recognize their religion faithfully reflected there. The Nation of Islam is fundamentalist in a way that Islam as a whole is not. Just by being in America, Islam can be adjusted from within by what surrounds it.

The rise of Christian fundamentalism to political prominence, especially in the United States, is something that should worry people all over the world. Especially in the southern states it is a potent force, and no month passes without it gaining more influence in towns and cities, legislatures and colleges. Liberals can easily pick holes in the fundamentalists' notion that the Bible cannot err. ('*Which* Bible is inerrant? And in *which* translation?' asks the theological liberal, while leaning back in his chair and paring his fingernails.) Yet fundamentalism is a multi-billion-dollar industry in North America, and the New Christian Right has certainly shown itself to be politically effective in Washington, DC, as well as in many state capitals. Fundamentalism is the fast food of American religious life, but for many it feeds an appetite for certainty in a world that is increasingly uncertain. It is the fundamentalists' unshakable trust in a biblical narrative that features the Battle of Armageddon fought in a Middle East not unlike the one we see on the news that sends a shudder down the spine. What frightens is not a hidebound approach to scripture but the combination of millennialism, dogmatism and access to military might. For a safer world, it would be better to expect those who aspire to the Senate and the Congress, let alone the Oval Office, to get a decent training in theology rather than in law or business studies.

Fundamentalism reached one height in the 1920s, in the northern states before the southern states, and after a lull it has started to peak once again. It is quickly becoming the central religious phenomenon of postmodern times. You can see it as a reaction to our world of relativity and anxiety, of cultured nihilism and irony. Yet it is a more complex phenomenon than most liberals are willing to credit. We fail to do it justice if we think only of the 'Monkey Trial' in Dayton, Tennessee, in 1925; we need to see its roots in American revivalism and to acknowledge that it has given hope to many people. In the hymns, prayers, readings and sermons of the churches, fundamentalism is the closest that many men and women get to having poetry in their lives. Of course, few people these days like to think of themselves as fundamentalists: they prefer to see themselves as Evangelicals or Pentecostals. *Other* people are fundamentalist, in much the same way as *other* people have ideologies. And lest it be thought that fundamentalism is something restricted to the poorly educated and the superstitious, I should say that it numbers more than a few scientists among its adherents. In a different formation, it can be found in an equally virulent form among the most highly educated people in society. I refer to the partisans of political correctness. If you *know* the truth, and *know* that certain books will impede the dissemination of that truth, and accordingly seek to remove those titles from curricula and school libraries, then you are a fundamentalist. You may call yourself a feminist or a Marxist, but you are also a fundamentalist.

Another aspect of religion today is syncretism. It is in evidence in Latin America where many Christian communities have fused elements of local religions. Some Haitians, for instance, attend mass with an exemplary piety while also practicing voodoo. They blend Catholic belief in resurrection with African belief that the souls of the dead rise to the stars. Or, with more difficulty, they hold together a belief in Jesus and Mary and the power of Legba and Erzulie. Postmodern syncretism in the first world differs from this phenomenon only insofar as it is influenced by a sense of the past as an archive and the present as a supermarket. Some believers have no interest in subscribing to an entire system of dogmas and prefer instead to mix and match their beliefs and practices. They might attend an Episcopal church yet feel quite comfortable folding in meditative practices drawn from Zen Buddhism, adding fringe liturgies devoted to goddess worship, or incorporating spiritual teachings of New Age gurus. In the first centuries of the Common Era many Christian communities were syncretistic, and now we see that orientation returning under the guise of pluralism. One difference between then and now is that the early Church was trying to discover its identity while Christianity today is struggling to retain an identity.

* * *

All this is quite different from what I will call postmodern religion, a notion that is most often used with Christianity in mind. Postmodern ideas of scripture are sometimes drawn from Judaism – in particular, from Kabbalistic, Midrashic and Talmudic styles of commentary – but when grafted onto Christianity they tend to have other senses and functions than in Judaism. As a placing shot, I will say that postmodern Christianity is an open set of attempts to rethink the faith by reference to those figures associated, rightly or wrongly, with postmodernism. Unlike fundamentalism, postmodern Christianity aims to be sophisticated with regard to literature and philosophy. If fundamentalism gives short shrift to the immense intellectual heritage of the faith, some postmodern Christians run the risk of bypassing revelation and reducing the faith to ethics with a few ancient stories attached. Having said that, I would like to sketch a few broad positions forged by postmodern theologians.

First of all, you can find proponents of a postmodern a/theology. Mark C. Taylor (1945–), for one, emerges from the 'death of God' school, whose most notable representative is Thomas J.J. Altizer (1927–). For Taylor, as for Altizer, the idea of a transcendent personal deity has become incredible, and Christianity must finally embrace atheism as its last and most challenging possibility. Nietzsche was right: God *is* dead. Yet he did not realize that this brings us closer to Jesus of Nazareth and his teaching of the Kingdom, now understood by way of ethics rather than revelation. Altizer takes this collapse of belief in a stable, transcendent order beyond our ken to mean that the immanent world about us is one of total presence. Sympathetic to the first move, Taylor has learned too much from Derrida about the allure of presence to agree with Altizer's conclusion. The world about us, nature and culture, may be all there is, but it is a play of difference and deferral, not full presence. European philosophers such as Hegel and Nietzsche and a poet such as William Blake are certainly needed to help define our contemporary situation. Altizer is surely correct there, Taylor thinks, although we can better elucidate our situation by examining popular culture. Let's look to Las Vegas sooner than Berlin, Jena or Paris: such is one burden of his recent work. No one can seriously believe in the God of the Nicene Creed, Taylor implies, and to that extent he affirms atheism. Yet there are traces of the sacred and of belief in our world, and we radically misinterpret it if we do not attend to them, and so it is more satisfactory to talk of a/theism rather than theism or atheism.

Far removed from a/theology is the school of radical orthodoxy, the most authoritative voice of which comes from John Milbank (1952–). Here there can be no question of jettisoning Nicene orthodoxy. On the contrary, that religious vision is to be preserved, and we can best clear room for it by way of a withering critique of modernity and its tireless will to secularism. The postmodern offers us hope to the extent that it is the post-secular, and religion is no longer to be brought before the court of science. Yet the postmodern is to be combated to the extent that, with Derrida and Foucault, it has shown itself to be in step with modern nihilism. Postmodernism follows one law, 'Thou shalt produce difference', with the consequence that we live in a state of perpetual transgression, about as far as possible from a land of peace. When understood correctly, though, the postmodern allows us to recover much of the premodern. In particular, we can regard St Augustine as a distant mirror.

Only a Trinitarian theology will overcome the finite, static world bequeathed to us by the Enlightenment, and that theology leads us ineluctably to a participatory ontology, the outlines of which were first drawn by Christian Neoplatonists. No longer a fussy old thing that sits quietly by itself in a corner, going 'Tut-tut' or doling out thin soup, theology should be assuming a robust cultural role. For Taylor, radical orthodoxy is a reactionary movement, while for Milbank a/theology is anemic liberalism. I will return to Milbank in the following chapter.

It can also be argued that, when they are read properly, Heidegger and Derrida do not develop arguments against the possibility of theology but against the viability of metaphysics, understood as the metaphysics of presence. These thinkers indicate the way to elaborate a non-metaphysical theology. That is, they help us to free God from the conception of him as remote and timeless, the ground of being or the being of beings. To worship that deity is no different from idolatry. This theology would not be a wholly new interpretation of Christianity, far from it: this late in the history of Christianity, the idea of a 'new theology' verges on self-contradiction. Yet there can be original theologies, movements that seek to recreate Christianity by returning to the wellsprings of the faith. In that spirit, we can distinguish positive and negative theologies in the writings of the Church Fathers. Positive theologies talk of God in terms of what is revealed by the Father in the Son through the Spirit. Negative theologies reflect critically on these statements, forever pointing out that predications made of God cannot naively use language that is appropriate to the world. Negative theologies are always braided with positive theologies. Two of the main architects of negative theology – Denys the Areopagite (fifth or sixth century) and Meister Eckhart (c.1260–1327), for example – do not elaborate theologies that are totally without metaphysics. There is often a Neoplatonic element in their writings, a sense of a deity whose being or non-being abides above all things, a pure self-presence that human tongues cannot describe in positive terms. With the help of Heidegger and Derrida, that metaphysics of presence in the writings of Denys and Eckhart can be identified and deconstructed, opening new ways of thinking and living the faith.

The view I have just outlined describes my early writing, and I have presented it directly instead of implying it in comments about other people's positions. My view differs from (a)theology in that it remains firmly oriented to Nicene orthodoxy, and differs from radical orthodoxy in two main ways. Rather than sharply separating modernity and postmodernity, I retain the narratives of liberty and the limits of liberty that are told so powerfully by modern thinkers, Marx and Freud among them, and I resist any attempt to reduce Christianity to a modification of Neoplatonism. Unlike Milbank, I do not take Derrida to be a nihilist or cast all modern thinkers as nihilists. However, I think that theological issues, when they come up in Derrida's writings, are always framed in philosophical ways, and that this tendency skews how those issues are presented within the faith. For Derrida, God is always to be thought in terms of undivided self-presence, and the concept is to be undone by reference to difference or, more precisely, *différance*. Yet the doctrine of the Trinity is based on differences between the three divine personæ, and the doctrine of Jesus as the Christ also turns on a difference, for the God-man has two natures that are not fused. What does 'difference' mean in these doctrines? Does it resemble *différance*? If so, what consequences follow? These are some of the questions that would guide a theology informed by deconstruction.

I would say that the deconstruction of Christianity reaches an internal limit, if only because it has derived some of its central insights from Judaism and Christianity. Derrida's word *déconstruction* is a reworking of *Destruktion*, a notion that Heidegger developed partly by way of Martin Luther's sense of *destructio* as presented in the *Heidelberg Disputation* (1518). Luther comes up with the word *destructio* when quoting Paul, 'I will destroy the wisdom of the wise' (1 Cor. 1:19), who in turn is quoting Isaiah 29:14. Of course, 'deconstruction' has other heritages, not the least important of them being the procedure that discloses how a poem is written. *Déconstruire*, 'to deconstruct', is a verb used long before Derrida started to write. It was once used to denote a way of seeing how poems work. If we suppress the meter of a poem by Baudelaire or Hugo we can get a better glimpse of its other structures. To the extent that this sense of the word is retained in Derrida's work, it indicates an interest in the poetics of discourse, how metaphysical motifs have been folded and refolded in a poem, a novel, an essay in philosophy, or a body of art criticism. So we must conclude that the word 'deconstruction' participates in the context of Jewish-Christian religiosity without simply belonging to it. That is enough for us to recognize that a deconstruction of Christianity would not mark an untroubled exit from the faith. It might even revivify the faith.

There are other original and fecund contributions to post-modern theology. I will consider the work of Jean-Luc Marion (1946–) in the next chapter, along with some of John Milbank's writings. Here, though, let me simply name Michel de Certeau (1925–86) whose *The Mystic Fable* (1982) helps to reconfigure our understanding of the mystical in the sixteenth and seventeenth centuries, and Louis-Marie Chauvet whose massive *Symbol and Sacrament* (1987) begins by deconstructing the old metaphysics that first determined the Catholic doctrine of the sacraments. I cannot consider his tome here, no more than I can pay attention to any of the remarkable writings that, with hindsight, seem to anticipate aspects of postmodern theology, treatises such as Pavel Florensky's *The Pillar and Ground of the Truth* (1914) where eternity is glimpsed through the cracks of human rationality, and Franz Rosenzweig's *The Star of Redemption* (1921) with its bold affirmation of the play of God, world and human being. Instead, I will introduce Derrida's recent work on religion.

* * *

In Derrida's first maturity as a writer, in the period of *Of Grammatology* (1967) and *Writing and Difference* (1967), he was commonly regarded as an atheist and, in the United States, as a Godless Nietzschean whose aim was to erode confidence in the Almighty. If we move forward about thirty years, Derrida is now approached, especially in the United States, as an advocate of ethics as infinite responsibility, a philosopher who broods on negative theologies, a man who ponders the sacred, a thinker of hospitality and forgiveness. What has happened?

One answer is 'Nothing at all'. Another is 'Rather a lot'. The first answer is plausible because Derrida, unlike most philosophers of his stature, has rarely changed his mind about a topic. Without a doubt, one finds scant attention to constructing an ethics or a philosophy of religion in his early writings. There are even doubts, like those that Heidegger ventured in his 'Letter on Humanism' (1947), whether one can develop an ethics free of metaphysics, and a general impression given that God is a point of pure self-presence and is therefore a metaphysical dream. Yet when we come to see what Derrida actually says about ethics and religion in his later work it would be mistaken to say that he has changed his mind in any significant respect. His reservations about ethics are taken seriously in his later writings (although he now sees a way of rethinking them), and he remains convinced that there is no God. As he says in 'Circumfession' (1991), he quite rightly passes for an atheist.

So how can it possibly be true that a lot has changed? The answer turns on a dialogue between Derrida and Lévinas. In *Writing and Difference* (1967) Derrida presented a close reading of *Totality and Infinity* (1961) that was deeply sympathetic in general and sharply critical at particular points. On Derrida's reading, Lévinas was caught in the tradition from which he had sought to escape. He was far closer to Hegel than he imagined himself to be, even when arguing against him; he had misunderstood key passages in Husserl and Heidegger, the main representatives of the phenomenological school to which he belonged; and he had uncritically prized speech over writing. Yet Lévinas responded to these criticisms and produced an astonishing book, *Otherwise than Being or Beyond Essence* (1974). Here is a work that Derrida found compelling, a text that although developed in a quite different idiom from Derrida's was one to which he could subscribe in his own way. That way was elaborated in terms of an aporia between the calculable and the incalculable, between law and justice.

An aporia? It is an ancient word, used by Aristotle in his discussion of time in the *Physics*, though one that has been revived in recent decades. It indicates the petering out of a pathway: reasoning has got us this far, and now there is nowhere else to go. For Derrida, the word denotes an irresolvable tension between incommensurables. Here is one of his examples. Law is a program: it brings the individual before laws that are wholly general ('You have broken the law; the penalty is five years in jail, without any exceptions'). Justice, however, can never be programmed: the individual case always exceeds the generality of the law ('You have broken the law; yet you did not intend to do anything wrong, you have been a decent citizen, you have dependents who need you to bring home an income, going to jail will do you more harm than good ...'). Justice, if there is such a thing, occurs in the experience of an aporia between the program and what cannot be programmed. It is an *experience*, never a resolution; and the judge, if he or she is just, never has a clear conscience because he or she never *knows* if the right act has been performed. Stepping back from all of this, we might say that Derrida has proposed a discourse on ethics that turns on *différance*, and so nothing has changed. And religion? The only shift is that Derrida started to attend closely to the topic, first of all responding to criticisms that deconstruction is a covert negative theology and then meditating on the state of religion today. I will take these one at a time.

As I said a moment ago, Christian theology properly consists of a doubled movement. Positive theologies are concerned with revelation: the Father is revealed in the Son through the Spirit. In positive theology, we attend to scripture and develop doctrines of the Christ and the Trinity. We ponder creation, fall and redemption. More generally, we seek to know God as the ground of beings. Negative theologies critically reflect on positive theologies, forever affirming the transcendence of God, and seeking to ensure that when we talk of God we are indeed talking of *God*, and not an idol. The disparity between creation and the Creator is so vast, the negative theologian insists, that we cannot compare the Creator to anything at all, not even to the entire cosmos. From the perspective of negative theology, all positive theology is enthralled by metaphysics to a greater or lesser extent. It figures the deity as the first being, the ground of being, or the being of beings, and thereby attempts to explain how things are. Denying that we can render the infinite deity intelligible to ourselves, the negative theologian severely questions the adequacy of each and every predicate that is given to God. This does not give us a *better* knowledge of God. Instead, by a movement of unknowing, one ascends to the deity and after many a trial is ecstatically united with the deity beyond all being.

We glanced at Derrida's first essay on negative theology, 'How to Avoid Speaking' (1989), at the end of the previous chapter. There we noted that, for him, pure prayer must be an address to the Other, and that Christian prayer – to the Father, Christ, the Spirit – is always impure because the Other has been named and thereby brought within a horizon of expectation. It is worth noting, just in passing, that there are times when Derrida affirms impurity: there is always generic and textual contamination, he argues. Yet there are other times when he endorses purity – religion without religion, pure prayer – and they occur whenever he talks about religion. Now, though, we should consider the charge that Derrida develops in deconstruction a new mutation of negative theology. On the face of it, the claim seems wildly mistaken. For if negative theology is an attempt to approach the transcendent, ineffable deity, it should be clear that Derrida, who rightly passes for an atheist, is not writing a negative theology. Derrida will tell us that God is always a moment of pure self-presence, hyper-essential being, and that such a reliance on presence is precisely what he proposes to deconstruct. And before we go on, we should take a moment or two to see if he is correct to say that.

As I said a little while ago, whenever Derrida talks about God he does so with one or more philosophical frames in mind. These frames are partial, to be sure, and in a certain way they are unavoidable. It might be possible to develop a theology that is not grounded in metaphysics: Albrecht Ritschl (1822–89) and Adolf von Harnack (1851–1930) sought to do precisely that, as did their fierce opponent on other issues, Karl Barth (1886–1968). But not even Barth thought it possible or even desirable to elaborate a theology that does not engage with philosophy. Arguments and concepts are needed in any discourse that claims intellectual respectability. In practice, Barth passed the bound set by that minimal criterion: a careful reader can find moments in the *Church Dogmatics* that are thoroughly Hegelian in character. From the fact that theology is partly framed by philosophy, however, it does not follow that theological remarks about God can be reduced to philosophical theses. One thing that skews Derrida's comments on God by philosophers in the Christian tradition is the absence of any theological understanding of the word and concept. To say that God is One is both a theological and a philosophical remark. To say that God is Trinity is a theological proposition that baffles all philosophers who are not Christian (and some who are). We might need philosophical concepts to help clarify it, insofar as it can be rendered intelligible, but it cannot be translated without crippling loss into the language of philosophy. And unless you conceive God as triune you are not talking about the Christian deity. To figure God as the eternal dance of Father, Son and Spirit, forever exceeding any limit, is not to settle on a moment of absolute self-presence. A difference is at the heart of the Christian God, and without that difference we cannot understand the deity as love.

My sense is that Derrida objects to God only when the deity is brought into philosophical discourse as the ground of being, the being of beings, the first being and the end of being. Yet he often gives the impression that the God of the Christians could always be reduced to the God of the philosophers. Either way, there can be no question of Derrida developing a negative theology that involves the deity. But is there another way in which a negative theology, or something resembling it, can be generated? There is. From his earliest writings, Derrida has been fascinated by *la différance*, the meaningless play of difference and deferral that he finds at work in both speech and writing. No one can present *différance* as such; it always withdraws behind words, and of course it does not exist in any sense of the word. It is a condition of possibility for any statement to be uttered, and at the same time it is a condition of impossibility that any statement can remain self-identical. (William Carlos Williams can write 'This Is Just To Say', a poem in the form of a note about eating cold plums from the fridge that his wife had kept for her breakfast; yet its lines can be reworked by Kenneth Koch to make his hilarious 'Variations on a Theme by William Carlos Williams', in which preposterous justifications are given for chopping down a house, giving away money, killing flowers and breaking a person's leg.) Derrida talks of *différance* as quasi-transcendental, by which he means that it can never form a stable ground although it always conditions our speech and our writing.

Différance is therefore not a master name for the hidden depths of reality, although a careless reader can sometimes get that impression from Derrida. At best, it is a nickname for the endless play of differing and deferring, one nickname among many others: *khôra*, *parergon*, *supplément*, and *trace*, being some of the more common. To talk about this spacing that always withdraws behind words in a poem or an essay requires similar moves to those the negative theologian makes about God. But the deconstructionist and the theologian have different aims in mind. We cannot talk properly of God because the deity transcends us, and we cannot talk adequately of *différance* because it is quasi-transcendental. Christians believe that God is radically other than us and yet (because of God's humanity) radically like us, so that when we pray we address the Other who is not other. Derrida is attuned to this, and maintains that *différance* or *khôra* has no human qualities; it is utterly foreign to us, it does not even exist, and yet it impinges on us. To address it is to call to the Other, and this is what Derrida has in mind when he talks about prayer being pure only when it is a response to the Other.

On one occasion Derrida addresses *la trace*, calling her 'Cinders', and the text he writes about her, *Cinders* (1982), is hauntingly beautiful. There are times when he seems to talk, almost in prayerful tones, to *khôra*. And perhaps the love letters that comprise the first part of *The Post Card* (1980) are all finally addressed to *la différance*. These are literary ploys, it will be said, perhaps used to make serious philosophical points but without any hope or expectation of communicating something to anyone. Cinders and Khôra do not hear us when we call to them. Yet when in *The Gift of Death* (1992), Derrida ventures the proposition *tout autre est tout autre*, which might be rendered, a little clumsily, as 'every other person is other in every way', there can be no doubt that singular human beings are being presented to us, individuals who can hear what we say to them. Is Derrida therefore suggesting that when we talk to another person we are addressing sheer otherness and that our communication, strictly understood, would be prayer? And does the idea even make sense?

* * *

At first blush, to say that you are completely other than me in all respects is highly implausible. I look at you and see that you resemble the image I have of myself in the mirror, at least to the extent that we both have heads, torsos and, in most cases, arms and legs. When you get a headache, you grimace more or less as I do when I am afflicted by the same malady. I know that you will die, just as I know that I am mortal. There is, we would agree, an analogy that binds my being to yours. Yet philosophers the caliber of Ludwig Wittgenstein in his *Philosophical Investigations* (1953) and Peter Strawson in his *Individuals* (1959) have poured cold water on this argument from analogy. It simply does not establish a sufficiently convincing case. When you get a headache you might not grimace, you might suffer it in silence or you might have to lie down for several hours. I cannot know what is going on in your mind by analogy with any degree of certainty. Also, my analogic knowledge of other minds is based solely on *my* experience, and that is a very small platform on which to build a towering theory.

Derrida does not draw on the objections of these analytic philosophers. Instead, he learns from two thinkers in the phenomenological tradition. Edmund Husserl argued in the fifth of his *Cartesian Meditations* (1931) that I am unable to grasp your stream of thoughts without thinking them for myself, and that would of course cancel your alterity at a stroke. Husserl's lectures were first published in French, translated by Lévinas who was later to inflect his teacher's point in his own way. You remain other than me, not because I cannot tell what you are thinking but because, in the social world, you address me from a height and call me to act responsibly towards you. That responsibility is, as we have seen, infinite. You and I abide in a relation without relation, and consequently there is no way in which I can fix a limit to my obligation to you. I sit at my laptop and work ceaselessly, and no matter how clearly I write, how apt my examples are, or how intensely I reread the authors whose views I am presenting and criticizing, I cannot say to myself 'Now I have done enough'. I can always do more for you, even if I have never met you and never will. Such is one thought that Lévinas offers to me.

When Derrida says *tout autre est tout autre* he speaks as someone who has inherited Lévinas's ethical spin on Husserl's insight. You are infinitely other than me, a unique and absolutely singular being; no matter how well I might know you, you will remain profoundly inaccessible to me. Lévinas would say that you are an enigma that interrupts my being, and not a phenomenon. Or, more exactly, if I begin to regard you as a phenomenon – by saying to myself, for example, 'What nice green eyes she has' – then I am no longer entirely regarding you ethically but am subsuming you in my gaze. Derrida would not disagree, although he does not restrict himself, as Lévinas does, to human beings. My cat is an absolutely singular being, he would readily admit, and so, in a sense, is the local eco-system in which I live. The question is, how does Derrida reach the conclusion that you are an absolutely singular being?

By way of reading Kierkegaard's *Fear and Trembling* (1843), is the short answer, and a longer one is coiled within it. Kierkegaard broods over the *Akedah*, Abraham's binding of his son Isaac in Genesis 22, which for the Danish philosopher is the prime example of a man leaving the ethical for the religious sphere. In obeying God's call to sacrifice his only son, Abraham suspends ethics: he elects to be responsible only to the absolute Other. His decision is wholly responsible, Derrida says; for to say 'Here I am' when the other person calls is the very instance of responsibility, as Lévinas has argued. Yet Abraham's decision is also madly irresponsible: how could he justify sacrificing his son to Sarah, his wife, to his community, let alone to Isaac? Here, surely, is someone who has abandoned the realm of the ethical and opened himself wholly to the charge of irresponsibility.

Derrida's strong twist on Kierkegaard's presentation of the *Akedah* is that it is not an extraordinary event but, on the contrary, a downright ordinary one. At this moment I am called to respond to you, in writing this book and in making it as good as it can be. In doing that, though, I am not playing with my daughters, not helping my wife clean the house, not campaigning to protect the local environment, not working in the shelter for the homeless in South

Bend, the city where I live, and so on. Merely by writing this book, by offering myself as a guide to postmodernism, I am making a massive sacrifice of other people, those I love and those I will never know, other animals and the fragile ecology of the world my children will inherit. This chair and this desk are my Mount Moriah. More to the point, I am sacrificing *ethics* understood as a realm of moral programs and calculable duties. Derrida tells me that my relation to you, dear reader, is not so much ethical as religious. Or, more exactly, he argues that I cannot really tell whether in writing this book, in talking to you for an hour or two a day, I am being ethical or religious. All that I know is that in attending to you, as other, I am not responding to the endless number of others, human and non-human, who call to me for help in any number of ways.

Having recast Abraham's situation as ordinary, not extraordinary, and thereby made all of our lives inescapably tragic, Derrida performs another twist. For Kierkegaard's Abraham, God is the figure of the wholly other. But if I treat someone – you, for example – as the wholly other then I am in effect regarding you as God. In addressing you, o unknown reader, I am as it were praying to the Wholly Other. *Tout autre est tout autre*: every other person is other in every way. As I repeat it to myself, this strange sentence seems to tell me that I can find God everywhere, in talking to anyone at all, and perhaps especially to you since you never disclose yourself to me. And at the same time it implies that at each and every moment I sacrifice God. Christians of a certain piety will say that they find the suffering Christ in the homeless in the city streets, in the African Americans on death row, and in the kid on crack who breaks into your house in the hope of finding some ready cash. Sometimes they will accuse themselves of crucifying Jesus each and every day of their lives, perhaps for doing no more than walking past a homeless woman on a cold street corner. Derrida would not use the same words as these folk but his implication runs in the same general direction as theirs.

And yet most Christians will be skeptical of Derrida's argument. Let me put a little pressure on just one point. Is it right to think of you and God as wholly other in exactly the same way? Is there no difference when I address God in prayer and when I address you when writing this book? Surely there is. Derrida tells me that you are absolutely singular, meaning that you are unique, irreplaceable and therefore infinitely precious. And so you are. Yet, slightly adapting a distinction drawn by the Swiss theologian Hans Urs von Balthasar

(1905–88), I would say that you and I are relatively singular, because, like all humans and all animals and all places, we are created beings. (It is our *similarity* not just our difference that makes us sympathize with others, we might say, echoing David Hume: we can imagine how the other person suffers.) Of humans, only Jesus is absolutely singular, for only Jesus, the God-man, has been born of the virgin and has been resurrected from the dead. It is Jesus's divinity that makes him singular. And we can bring that into sharp focus by noting that only God is *absolutely singular*. Only he exists absolutely of himself.

* * *

Tout autre est tout autre: when I whisper those five words to myself now I hear Derrida telling me that my sense of God as the Wholly Other derives from my prior discovery of your otherness. Notice that Derrida is not developing a case against religion. He is arguing two things at once. First, he maintains that the line separating ethics and religion is divided and equivocal. When I attend to you and say 'Here I am', I do not know with any certainty if I am being ethical or religious. For when I treat you as the other I minimally accord you the status of being like God, even if I happen to be an atheist. And second, dogmatic religion is an edifice built on a prior faith that I can share with even those who reject the dogmas to which I sub-scribe. Derrida calls this faith religion without religion. It is, as he says in *The Gift of Death*, a philosophical doublet of dogmatic reli-gion, and it is characterized by a thinking of the possibility of revela-tion but is not burdened by having to believe in what derives from an actual event of revelation.

The expression 'religion without religion' employs the syntax that we have come to associate with Maurice Blanchot: *X* without *X*. When Blanchot talks of a relation without relation, he has in mind the transcendence that the other person has with respect to me, and that I have with respect to him or her. And when Derrida speaks of religion without religion, this sense is preserved. To prize the *ethical* transcendence of the other person will generate a religion without religion, namely a faith that can be developed without reference to *religious* transcendence: the aseity or self-generation of the deity or the ecstasy achieved by the soul in its ascent to God. What happens if we transform Christianity into a religion without religion? We would have a faith in which the Incarnation, Resurrection and Ascension of Jesus are possible events but are not obligatory for anyone to affirm. Christianity would develop without needing to be answerable to the Nicene Creed. We cannot fairly say that the faith has been reduced to ethics, for, as we have seen, we have no indubitable knowledge whether our actions are ethical or religious. None of this would make Christianity a natural religion although it would make it universal in principle. It would be marked by faith but a faith in what is to come and not a faith deriving from what has already taken place.

Judaism, Christianity and Islam: these three Abrahamic religions all reflect on events that are believed to have occurred in history. Derrida calls them messianic faiths. It can be objected that none of these faiths is an undivided reflection on historical events: each is oriented to the future. Jews await the Messiah, and while Christians believe that Jesus is the Messiah we also look for the eschatological fulfillment of his life, suffering and death. That said, all the Abrahamic religions are concerned with a past that was once present, the present moment, and a future that will be present. Religion without religion would be a faith without the messianic, it would not depend on any of those religions or any others like them. In a recent essay, 'Faith and Knowledge: The Two Sources of "Religion" at the Limits of Reason Alone' (1996), Derrida dubbed the structure of this old-new faith 'messianicity'. We can best view this structure by returning to a topic that has already concerned us in an earlier chapter: experience. Plainly, experience is far more general than any of the Abrahamic religions, or any others you might care to name. I experience things, so does the rabbi at the local synagogue, and the Shi'ite Muslim on a pilgrimage to Mecca.

For Derrida, experience is not the reception and processing of a steady flow of events; it is exposure to the other. As soon as I sit at my laptop and begin writing another part of this book, I am promising to tell you the truth about postmodernism. With each word I write, I am silently assuring you that I am telling you the truth as I see it; and even if the devil got into me one morning and I tried to trick you by making you believe that Michel Foucault is an American analytic philosopher of science who teaches at Princeton and is also known for his signally fine stamp collection, I would still be quietly promising to tell you the truth. I cannot tell a lie without having made that promise. So I have faith that you will read my words with some care, and you have faith that I will not trick you. No sooner do I address you than I expose myself to the unforeseen. I might sit down at my desk again this evening and have an insight into the postmodern world that completely changes my attitude to it. Or, for all I know, you might write me a nasty letter or send me a photograph of yourself in the nude. Without the unforeseeable being a structural possibility of my guiding you around postmodernism, this would not be an experience for me.

Religion without religion is of a piece with democracy, Derrida argues. The faith that links singular individuals such as you and I is prior to any social bond or political arrangement that might be devised. It can be universalized, crossing the lines that separate Christians and Jews, Jews and Muslims, Muslims and Buddhists. As we saw in chapter three, Derrida argues that democracy is structured as a promise: there will always be more to be drawn from the concept. It is tempting to see in Derrida's culture of singularities in which all people are equal, regardless of gender or color, political affiliation or religious belief, a late version of what Jesus called the Kingdom of God. Of course, it will come as no surprise whatsoever if we have to modify that expression and say that it is the Kingdom of God without God.

* * *

On Derrida's analysis, religion without religion is not a wholly new phenomenon. One can see a faith that does not rely on institution and dogma emerging in philosophy since the Enlightenment. It is there in Hegel and Kierkegaard, in Heidegger and Lévinas, in Ricoeur and Marion. It is also there in Kant, and in many ways it begins in his *Religion within the Limits of Reason Alone* (1793) with its program of offering a reasonable, trim and moral interpretation of the faith. Actually, once you start to look for it you can find it long before people started to talk about modern times: in Meister Eckhart's homilies about the birth of the Word in the soul, and – if you squint a little – in St Augustine's suggestion at the end of the first book of *On Christian Doctrine* that the person who is mature in faith no longer needs scripture. Indeed, if you look hard enough at the Church Fathers, you can find points when Christianity is presented in part as a religion without religion: it has spiritualized all that was revealed to the Jews and thereby made it seem primitive, a perception that has generated enormous evil.

Turning to modern times, you can find more folk who might be seen to be foreshadowing religion without religion. Dietrich Bonhoeffer (1906–45), for one, argued for a Christianity come of age, a faith without religion. And Karl Rahner (1904–84), for another, urged us to accept a Christianity that relied on the vague and unthematic experience of God that occurs in acts of loyalty and sacrifice, love and toleration, and to see dogma as a structure built on top of that experience. For Rahner, a Buddhist or a Jew or a Muslim who had this transcendental experience of God but who was constrained by the dogmas of his or her faith is an implicit Christian or (even more problematically) an anonymous Christian. And of course the compliment, if it is one, goes in the other direction as well: a Christian of good faith is to be regarded by a Buddhist as an implicit or anonymous Buddhist. Doubtless many Christians will object that being a Christian is anything but anonymous, while a good Muslim, for example, will surely add that he or she doesn't want to be considered a Christian in any shape or form! Rahner will defend himself by saying that a Christian has no choice but to say that Christ redeems all who can be redeemed, regardless of their religious confession. Yet the sharpness of the responses to Rahner's notion of anonymous Christianity indicate just how difficult it is to construct an effective theology of religions.

Derrida's idea of religion without religion does not run into the same difficulties as Rahner's theology of religions. After all, it is an elaboration of what is taken to be prior to *any* positive religion, and consequently it does not rely on any dogmas, however liberally interpreted they may be. The problems with the theory are otherwise. To a Christian who prays, who participates in the liturgy and who lives a sacramental life, the notion of religion without religion seems bloodless and abstract. The particularity of the faith has been lost. Ethics is certainly an important part of the religious life, but it is far from being the whole story or even its motivation. People are religious because they have experience of the holy, or because they live and move and have their being within the dimension of faith. Jesus said that the second commandment is *like* the first commandment, religious folk will say, and while the implication is that no rigid line is to be drawn between adoration and ethics (the latter should follow from the former) the priority of worship is always to be maintained.

In the end what Derrida offers us in his philosophy of religion is yet another chapter in the story of religion that began with Kant. Or maybe the story begins far earlier, goes back as far as Heraclitus's fragment 199 that tells us that *ethos* is the proper dimension of the sacred. But let's not debate beginnings. We can agree that the story does not really grip Christian imaginations until it comes to be related by Kant. To be sure, Kant construed ethics by way of a universal moral law, and Derrida rejects that approach in favor of a culture of singularities that can in principle be universalized. Ethics is to be thought with reference to the incalculable, not just the calculable, the impossible and not only the possible. And the border between ethics and religion is shown to tremble. Yet the general approach is the same: reduce religion to ethics and a few ancient stories, approach the first commandment by way of the second. 'Reduce' can mean 'lead back', and Derrida surely believes that religion is grounded in ethics as infinite responsibility. But what we get is 'reduce' in the sense of 'to bring lower', in this case, to explain religious transcendence by way of ethical transcendence. For the Christian informed by a Trinitarian faith, it does not work: relative singularity is not absolute singularity.

Religions may be at the root of many wars, as Derrida rightly observes, and they may lead to all sorts of fanatical activity in war or peace. However, a believer will always argue that these are abuses of religion and that there is nothing that can be insulated from abuse. One can pray for peace before a cross. This is a good thing. Also, one can erect a twenty-six foot cross at Auschwitz, and thereby wound Jews who can no longer pray there. This is surely not a good thing. Further, as happened in May 1999, explosives can be placed under three hundred crosses at Auschwitz with the intent of killing those who remove them. This is an evil perversion of Christianity. Derrida would readily concede the point that anything can be abused, but he would not abandon his argument as a whole. For him, positive religion remains a danger, and even the most devout among us need to be reminded of that, in times of peace and especially in times of war.

further reading

Caputo, John D. *The Prayers and Tears of Jacques Derrida: Religion without Religion*. Bloomington: Indiana University Press, 1997.
——, ed. *The Religious*. Oxford: Basil Blackwell, 2002.
Derrida, Jacques. *The Gift of Death*, trans. David Wills. Chicago: University of Chicago Press, 1995.
Derrida, Jacques. 'Faith and Knowledge: The Two Sources of "Religion" at the Limits of Reason Alone', trans. Samuel Weber.

In Derrida and Gianni Vattimo, eds. *Religion*. Cambridge: Polity Press, 1998, 1–78.

Hart, Kevin. *The Trespass of the Sign: Deconstruction, Theology and Philosophy*, expanded edition. New York: Fordham University Press, 2000.

Taylor, Mark C. *Erring: A Postmodern A/Theology*. Chicago: University of Chicago Press, 1984.

Westphal, Merold, ed. *Postmodern Philosophy and Christian Thought*. Bloomington: Indiana University Press, 1999.

the gift: a debate

Most guides will assure you that the postmodern world is thoroughly secular. In this respect above all, they will say, you can see that the modern and the postmodern are in continuity. Look at the world around you: Los Angeles is no city of angels, and Jerusalem is no city of God. Modern atheism set down roots in the Enlightenment; those roots grew deeper in the nineteenth century; and after the Shoah no one can possibly believe in a benign deity. If God is all knowing, he knew what was happening at Auschwitz. If God is present everywhere, he was there. If God is supremely powerful, he could have prevented children, women and men from being routinely murdered. And if God is wholly good, he would surely have heard his people's cries for justice. The sheer fact that the Holocaust happened suffices to disprove that the God of Judaism and Christianity exists.

So say protest atheists, people who deny God on the basis of unmerited human suffering. Here is how their case plays out. If there *is* a God, he cannot be all knowing or almighty or always present or (more worryingly) all good. Take away whichever quality you like, but you cannot credibly assign all of them to God. Yet if you remove just one quality, you no longer have the God of your grandparents. You merely have a super-being who had been frustrated by the Nazis. Can anyone today believe in a *finite* God? That is one of the questions that protest atheists want you to answer. The other one, as you have probably guessed, is this: Can anyone today believe in an *infinite* God? Theodor W. Adorno (1903–69) famously pronounced that it was barbaric to write poetry after Auschwitz. In a related sense, protest atheists say that it is obscene to pray to the God of our grandparents once we have taken in the full horror of the Shoah.

One thing that those same guides should also tell you, though, is that there is no *one* postmodernity. It is salutary to remember that relations between the modern and the postmodern can be thought of in diverse ways. For some folk, the postmodern is an invitation to elaborate a way of being that is utterly post-secular. On this understanding, the postmodern would alert us to insufficiencies and problems in modernity: its reliance on static, spatial models of knowledge, its narrowly Ramist understanding of method, its heavy emphasis upon the solitary self, its stress upon disinterestedness, its impatience with ritual, and its willful confusion of mystery and mystification. Postmodern thinkers and those to whom they are close can show us ways of criticizing these tendencies in modernity, post-secularists will tell us. Some will point us to Heidegger or Derrida, others to Kierkegaard or Lévinas. Prudent and insistent voices will add that these thinkers themselves need to be criticized before they can be of much help to us. Take Heidegger, for instance. He is invaluable for diagnosing the metaphysics of presence in Western philosophy, but he was quite mistaken to suggest that it also structures Christian thought. St Thomas Aquinas does not figure God by way of a hardened presence in his account of God as *esse*, his act of being. Besides, Heidegger's later view that only poets are attuned to the possibility of a new manifestation of the holy is a Romantic dream, one that leads to the neo-pagan fantasy of the fourfold. In his final works Heidegger was taken with the idea of mortals, gods, earth and the heavens all participating in the dance of being. If the idea appeals to some people attracted to eco-spiritualism, it frightens others who centrally identify themselves as Jews, Muslims and Christians.

Anyone willing to think of the postmodern as the post-secular will surely point out that the word 'modernism' has two senses. I indicated this way back in the first chapter, and said then that I would use the word only in one sense until much later in the book. Well, it is time to bring both senses into play. Let me refresh your memory of what I said. 'Modernism' usually denotes the *avant garde* culture of the early twentieth century, and we associate it more or less loosely with artists like T.S. Eliot and James Joyce, Pablo Picasso and Piet Mondrian, Arnold Schoenberg and Erik Satie. When the word is used in discussions of religion, however, 'modernism' indicates a different set of names: Freidrich von Hügel and Alfrey Loisy, George Tyrell and Maurice Blondel, Ernesto Buanaiuti and Lucien Laberthonnière. These thinkers agreed more in their dissatisfaction with received theology than in any program that would replace it. Not all of them thought that religion springs from the unconscious, nor did all of them think that it is a matter of experience, nor indeed did they all agree that doctrine is no more than a series of dead metaphors. Yet all of them held at least one of those views, whether in a strong or a weak sense.

Some of the people who come after theological modernism, and who reject its liberal orientation, call themselves post-liberal theologians. The Yale Lutheran George A. Lindbeck is the most conspicuous of them, and his book *The Nature of Doctrine* (1984) has become their rallying point. Lindbeck develops a cultural-linguistic approach to religion, which is to say that he attempts to interpret doctrines as rules that make sense in a given culture. The theory is non-reductive, and he promotes it with the aim of facilitating ecumenical discussion: if the different churches could stop arguing about authority and metaphysics and look closely at the nature of doctrine, there would be more unity in Christendom. Liberalism has not succeeded in advancing ecumenical discussion because of its firm methodological commitment to doctrine as dead metaphors for feelings and attitudes, unconscious desires and orientations to being. If doctrines can change without a person's experience altering, or people's experience can vary without doctrines having to be rephrased, then liberalism will be too accommodating for any sensible discussion about unity in Christ.

If you take several steps away from Lindbeck's project, it begins to resemble Quine's web of belief. Like Quine, Lindbeck is an anti-foundationalist: there are no universal structures by which one can decide between religious and non-religious interpretations of reality, he admits. Also, he holds that some doctrines can be revised or at least given another scansion. The Immaculate Conception of the Virgin Mary, for example, is irreversible only if we are bound to a particular theology of creaturely freedom and a stern Augustinian theology of original sin. Should the Church modify its theology of original sin in important respects, the doctrine of the Immaculate Conception would become reversible. Of a piece with this general approach, Lindbeck maintains that the creeds of Nicea and Chalcedon should not be regarded as preserving permanent metaphysical truths about Christ and the Trinity. Rather, they should be read as identifying the paradigms by which it is possible to be a Christian. With respect to the creeds, Lindbeck is not out to deny, for example, that Christ and the Father have the one substance; and he certainly has no desire to revise or abolish the creeds: they are too deeply embedded in Christian cultures for that to be envisaged, even were it desirable. Instead, he wishes to argue that metaphysical statements such as the one just mentioned are not doctrinally binding. What counts, he thinks, is whether a person is conformed to Jesus Christ as he is represented in the biblical stories about him; and he points out that there are many ways in which this can be so.

Lindbeck calls himself a post-liberal rather than a postmodern theologian, although he does not reject the latter label out of hand. Like Rorty, he thinks that we live in a world of changing vocabularies: there is no 'final vocabulary' to be attained. People become Christian not because Christianity unequivocally makes better sense of 'being human' but for all sorts of reasons, admirable and less than admirable. Once they are inside the fold and have learned its language – one that turns on *sola scriptura*, say, or another that revolves around the sacraments – they can profess the faith. Like Derrida, Lindbeck glosses meaning in terms of an item's sense and function in an overarching sequence. Theological description is intra-semiotic, conditioned by the other signs that surround it, he argues. Perhaps he would approve a post-liberal sentiment phrased in Derrida's idiom such as 'Christianity always calls for more Christianity'. There is always more Christianity to be drawn from the stories about Jesus as the Christ and the creedal paradigms. The faith is not restricted to particular philosophical assumptions about 'substance', philosophical theories about 'relations', or theological theses about sin.

Yet there are major thinkers who are skeptical of theological modernism and who do not fit at all into postmodern theology, however generously it is conceived. To be postmodern you must mark a tension, if not a rupture, between the modern and your own thought. No one would think that Jürgen Habermas (1929–) is a postmodern critical theorist: he doggedly maintains that modernity is an unfinished project, and that in the interests of social justice and intellectual liberty it should be brought to completion. Similarly, Karl Rahner (1904–84), who made a fleeting appearance at the end of the last chapter, would not be properly identified as a postmodern theologian, even though he was dubious about some tendencies in theological modernism.

Why not? Not because he relied partly on the spirituality of St Ignatius Loyola (1493–1556), the founder of the Jesuits. A postmodern thinker can be linked to anyone or anything from the past. If anything, Rahner's Ignatian spirituality prevents him from being as modern as some of his critics believe he is. His emphasis on God as the Holy Mystery, which became more and more pronounced in his writings, cannot be reconciled with the God of philosophical modernity. Rahner is not postmodern because he relied, and heavily so, on a modern philosophy of the human subject, drawn from Descartes, refined by Kant and Husserl, and then cued into Thomist theology by Joseph Maréchal (1878–1944). It was Rahner's view that modern theology should be grounded in theological anthropology, that is, a theology of the human subject. In our ordinary acts of forgiveness and renunciation, in taking on responsibilities without the prospect of reward and in resigning ourselves to suffering, we transcend ourselves. This movement of self-transcendence occurs within an absolute horizon of being which Rahner does not hesitate to call God. Our quotidian experiences of each other therefore presume an oblique reference to God, and we are assured that those acts were always made possible by divine grace. To be sure, our everyday experience of God is vague; it is neither lit by the intellect nor focused by the emotions. Only very rarely do we derive consolation from this experience. It is more usual for us to bear our disappointments and our failures in silence, assured only that through them we are being quietly addressed by God. While Rahner makes us all minor mystics, he does not lead us to hope for the heights of spiritual joy.

From time to time Rahner found himself opposed by Hans Urs von Balthasar (1905–88), who countered Rahner's mysticism of everyday life with quite another understanding of the mystical. We do not experience God by fulfilling our highest possibilities, he argued, but by conforming ourselves to Christ. Our life with Christ is not a series of experiences but an experience of non-experience. Conservative as he came to seem, especially in ecclesial politics, von Balthasar nonetheless can be regarded as the most significant of all postmodern theologians. Far from accepting the claims of modernity, as represented by Descartes and Kant (and with Galileo in the background), von Balthasar radically rethinks what counts as modernity. The modern period, he tells us in the fifth volume of *The Glory of the Lord* (1965), begins much earlier than the seventeenth century, perhaps as early as the philosophy of the Islamic thinker Avicenna (980–1037). Certainly its roots can be found in the Averroism of the mid-thirteenth century. Averroës (1126–98) was an Arabic philosopher who lived in Spain, and the bulk of his work consists of commentaries on Aristotle. Translated into Latin in the century after his death, these commentaries exerted a powerful influence on some scholastic philosophers, to the disquiet of champions of orthodoxy such as St Albert the Great (c.1193–1280) and St Thomas Aquinas (c.1226–74). Especially worrying was the Averroist emphasis on the primacy of reason over faith, philosophy over theology. In the last analysis, revealed truths were of a lower status for the Averroists than the truths of reason.

To prize reason over faith was implicitly to close the gap between created beings and the Creator. For a later thinker such as Johannes Duns Scotus (c.1265–1309), the gap was effectively to be narrowed by determining a universal idea of being that could be predicated of both the finite and the infinite, humans and God. Contrary to what many critics say, Scotus did not contend that there is no difference between the being of God and the being of his creation. Only God exists by virtue of his essence, Scotus teaches, and we exist only because we participate in God. Without a universal idea of being, though, we could not prove the existence of God: we would always be in search of some way of holding together infinite and finite being in our minds. The Thomist school fiercely disagreed with the Franciscan teacher, and insisted that there is no universal idea of being, only an analogy of being between God and his creatures. Nonetheless, Scotus's view – or, let us say, a subtle misunderstanding of it – is the one that von Balthasar believes to have inaugurated the modern period. Whether intentionally or not, Scotus has encouraged many philosophers to regard *finite* being as the whole of being, and to forget infinite being, namely God. Indeed, the Scotist concept of being is quietly raised above God. No longer is being grasped as *reality*; it is itself grasped as a *concept*. The Almighty himself is expected to stand before the concept of universal, neutral and indeterminate being.

Scotus's view of being could well have been a historical oddity, one that was sidelined by the new and vibrant interests of the Renaissance, but, in von Balthasar's judgment, it survived the Renaissance and has had a subterranean yet vast influence on later thought. The idea of universal, indistinct, neutral being is rethought, refocused and massively elaborated by the Jesuit theologian Francisco Suárez (1548–1617) in his *Disputationes Metaphysicae*

(1597), the encyclopedic work from which most European philosophers learned their trade throughout the seventeenth century. For Suárez, the Scotist determination of being was the object of metaphysics, and to abandon the universal idea of being in favor of an analogy of being would be to jettison all the assurances that a rigorous metaphysics can give to us. Analogy is uncertain at best; the study of being leads us to certainty, including certainty about God. We know that Suárez's metaphysics significantly shaped Descartes's thought while he was studying with the Jesuits at La Flèche, and his philosophy passed on the tradition von Balthasar sketches to the modern age in the writings of Leibniz and Spinoza, Kant and Hegel, Husserl and Heidegger. It was Suárez who prepared the way for Descartes and Kant by teaching that being is a concept that can be grasped by reason. Now if being is a concept, then it belongs to a subject. And if that is so, we do not rely on the infinite being of God; rather, God must be situated with respect to our mental categories. Put this way, it is only a couple of short steps from Scotus to Kant. More generally, if we think of modernity as beginning with Descartes or one of his contemporaries (Shakespeare was older, Newton was younger), we have remained blind to the importance of Suárez, Scotus and Averroës. Worse, we have seriously underestimated the age of modernity and remained unaware of its theological significance.

It will come as no surprise to hear that von Balthasar seeks to affirm the transcendence of God, and the reality of the Trinity. He thereby calls into question the modernity that prizes reason over faith, being as a concept over the Almighty. One consequence of modernity, as we have seen, is the tendency to lead religion back to its purported ground in ethics. A robust postmodern faith, by contrast, would be oriented entirely to the love of God. To be turned to God is to be engulfed by an excessive love that cannot be appropriated by a human subject; it overflows your actions and your words. This is quite different from the model of ethics we inherit from Kant, in which we are all constrained by the moral law to be decent, upright citizens. And it is also different from the rethinking of this practical ethics by Lévinas and Derrida. The incalculable dimension of my response to you originates with God, not you. Christian love cannot be thought in terms of interpersonal relations – you and I, say – but instead by way of a response to the free gift of divine love. For Lévinas and Derrida we cannot strictly decide whether we are engaged with ethics or religion. For von Balthasar, however, it is imperative that we make a decision. It does not suffice to address myself to you as wholly other than me. The wholly other is God, and you are similar to him, although only in the overreaching context of a tremendous, humbling dissimilarity. In Derrida's argument that, from my perspective, you are like God because you are *tout autre* in every way, von Balthasar would discern not an analogy of being but the traces of the Scotist doctrine that there is a universal idea of being. The exemplary postmodern, as many like to see Derrida (much to his distaste), would thus become an exemplar of modernity.

Rather than exploring von Balthasar's theology in any more detail, I turn to two thinkers who have read him closely and who would not shy away from being called postmodernists. I choose Jean-Luc Marion (1946–) and John Milbank (1952–) partly because of their importance in contemporary intellectual culture and partly because Milbank has engaged Marion in debate on more than one occasion. Both Marion and Milbank are thinkers of the gift, and both have tried to rethink the modern subject. I will organize my reading of them around these twin themes.

* * *

Jean-Luc Marion's work mainly consists of three imposing triptychs: one that explores modernity, another devoted to theology, and yet another given to a phenomenology of givenness. The third triptych consists of *Reduction and Givenness* (1989), *Being Given* (1997) and *In Excess* (2001). The second: *The Idol and Distance* (1977), *God Without Being* (1982) and *Prolegomena to Charity* (1986). And the first: *Sur l'ontologie grise de Descartes* (1975), *Sur la théologie blanche de Descartes* (1981) and *On Descartes' Metaphysical Prism* (1986). Let's begin by considering the first triptych, the powerful interpretation of that foundational figure of philosophical modernity, René Descartes (1596–1650).

Throughout, but especially in the center panel, the study of Descartes's metaphysics, Marion attends to the philosopher's treatment of the ego and his conception of God. Is Descartes a metaphysical thinker? Certainly: he determines the ego as *cogitatio sui*, the being that thinks itself, and God as the *causa sui*, the being that causes itself. Is he simply a metaphysical thinker? No: his understanding of the ego and God indicate the limits of metaphysics and go beyond them. The ego is held to be free and to establish possibility as the first modality of being, while God is to be approached under the divine name of infinity: neither conception is neatly metaphysical. It is with these questions and these broad responses to them that Marion begins to rethink the nature and essence of philosophical modernity. His approach to Descartes's thought and the history of modern philosophy remains strictly phenomenological. In its broadest sense, that means he does philosophy in the wake of Husserl and Heidegger, and alongside older contemporaries such as Lévinas and Michel Henry (1922–2002). More narrowly, it means that his thought is oriented with respect to two ideas: the intentional structure of consciousness and the phenomenological reduction. These are ideas we need to know more about.

All consciousness is consciousness *of* something, Husserl maintained. All my psychic acts – cognitions, desires and dispositions – have objects, and these objects form a world with my consciousness as its center. It is not a passive center around which a world turns. Not at all: it has the character of an act. When I walk from home to my office, I do not pass a random series of objects: cars, houses, trees, trash bins on the sidewalk, a dog that barks at me, a woman out for a jog in the early morning, people queuing up for the first coffee of the day. No, I am continuously moving through a coherent world that is meaningful for me. I know when I pass a certain house that I am about half-way to work. I turn over thoughts for my seminar on Gerard Manley Hopkins that I will teach later in the day; I consider whether I have enough time to cross Cleveland Road before the lights change; I say 'Hi' to the jogging woman at more or less the right moment as she passes me; I turn over an idea about a chapter of this book; I mentally revise a stanza of a poem I have been writing; or I wish I had had a little more for breakfast. Sometimes I am taken away with a thought or a desire and find that I am almost at the university: I don't even remember walking under that bridge that goes over Juniper Road! My experiences are not arbitrary; they are a field of action that I negotiate by adjusting myself to them, engaging with them, or tuning out of them. I understand my world not by referring events to natural science ('The cardinal communicates an enormous amount of information about nearby food and danger to other birds through a brief whistle') but by being in relation to them (I say to myself, 'What a sweet song! I bet that's a cardinal'). Most of the time, while walking to work, I am aware of myself *both* perceiving this or that *and* being a subject engaging with the world, an 'I'.

In *Being Given* (1997), one of his later works, Marion will come to resituate the consequences of Husserl's doctrine of intentionality. In particular, he will thoroughly rethink the notion of the subject as transcendental – that is, forming the condition of possibility for experience – and yet he will claim that in doing so he remains faithful to phenomenology, perhaps even more faithful than Husserl was himself. Before we can get even the barest glimpse of all that, however, we need to grasp what Husserl means by the phenomenological reduction. We prepare to do phenomenology when we suspend the natural attitude, that is, when we no longer appeal to religion or science (or what gets washed up as 'common sense') as we habitually do when trying to make sense of our experience. Anything exterior to experience – anything *transcendent*, as Husserl puts it – must be bracketed, put out of play. This does not bring us to the brink of an irresponsible subjectivism; it leads us to consider the field of action of which we are a part from the position of being the *subject* of those acts. The suspension is called the phenomenological *epoché*, and it prepares us for the phenomenological reduction.

The word 'reduction' derives from a Latin verb (*re* + *ducere*, to lead) so it means 'to lead back'. I engage in phenomenology when I am led back to my experiences as they are actually lived by me. Let's take an example. I enter my study, and my eyes rest on a birthday card made for me several years ago by one of my daughters; it is propped against some of my books. Common sense tells me that it is just a piece of paper, colored with crayons, and with a picture of a kitten pasted in one corner. Now if I bracket common sense, I do not doubt that the card is made of paper, colored with crayons, and has sticky tape at the top. I do not doubt that it exists. What I deny is the commonsense assumption that the things of the world are constituted as meaningful before they enter my world of experience. So I engage with that card as an experience that unfolds. I see how it is a part of my world, my family and my work. I do not experience love as an abstract category, as is done in one of the philosophy books it half covers. No, I experience it as felt, as lived in a complex way, with ups and downs, with my daughters and my wife. As I let the experience unfold in its own way and in its own time, my experiences as a child, with a father of my own, also comes to light. They are situated on my intentional horizon, and perhaps now I am a father myself I can make better sense of some of them. I see how my experience as a child and my child's experience of me pass into each other, setting up extremely complex movements inside myself.

Throughout all this, I appeal to nothing outside to make sense of my experience for me. Instead, I let the experience unfold itself, become intelligible to me, in all the concreteness of the ordinary occasion.

Descartes, you will remember, doubted the existence of the world in his *Meditations on First Philosophy* (1641). He thought that he should strip away all his habitual beliefs in order to find an unshakable ground, which he found and thoroughly examined – but did not name – in the second meditation. (The well-known expression *cogito ergo sum*, 'I think therefore I am', appears in the fourth part of the *Discourse on Method*, in *The Principles of Philosophy* and in *The Search After Truth*.) He discovered that he could not doubt that he was actually thinking. Having achieved that absolute certainty, he assured himself that God exists and that God would not deceive him; and then he was able to rebuild his world, this time on firm foundations. Modern European philosophy begins with Descartes. His work has been accepted as a model of rigor, and that work itself prizes mathematics as the ideal of rigor. Descartes's writing is also a standard of clarity. French devotion to *la clarté*, and French rebellion against it, are equally responses to the prose of the *Discours de la méthode* and the *Meditationes de prima philosophie*.

In 1929, when Husserl presented the thought of his last maturity at the Sorbonne in Paris, he started by paying homage to the man he recognized as France's preeminent thinker, Descartes. The expansion of those two lectures was later published as *Cartesian Meditations* (1950). Yet Husserl is quite unlike Descartes: his interest is not in whether the world truly exists but in how it becomes meaningful. Nor does he disclose a pure *cogito*, removed from the world. The Husserlian subject is always and already in touch with objects. As we have seen, consciousness is intentional in structure. And yet consciousness can detach itself and reflect on those objects and examine how they are related to it. If we perform the *epoché* and the reduction, we can see how we are related to our objects of consciousness. We can regard them as concretely situated with respect to our intentional horizon, which changes over time, and we can thereby unfold their full meaning in terms of our shifting desires, feelings and thoughts. Dry and formidable as Husserl's prose is, phenomenology nonetheless attracts those artists and poets who hear about it out of school. Francis Ponge (1899–1988) is one such poet, as his prose poems from *Taking the Side of Things* (1942) to *Soap* (1967) attest, and Charles Simic (1938–) is another, as his cheeky

meditations on ordinary things like forks and shirts and pencil stubs
make delightfully clear. Some artists are influenced by phenomenology, whether directly or indirectly; others simply find there a sympathetic understanding of artistic creation. Perhaps it is the image
of the poet about to begin writing or the painter picking up a brush
that best suggests to us what the *epoché* is.

The history of phenomenology is a history of the creative
rethinking of intentionality and reduction. For all intents and
purposes, Heidegger dropped the reduction and explored intentionality with respect to *Dasein* (human being as situated in the world,
its 'being there') rather than continuing to think of a subject
animated by consciousness. Maurice Merleau-Ponty (1908–61)
argued that it is the failure of the reduction that is most instructive in
doing phenomenology. Lévinas objects to the reduction as an old-
fashioned theoretical gesture given a make-over, yet retains
intentional analysis; while Paul Ricœur (1913–) proposes to add
hermeneutics, the theory of interpretation, to phenomenology in
order to prevent it from lapsing into subjective idealism. Derrida
seeks to preserve the reduction yet maintains that it is never entirely
successful: it is always and already deferred and delayed by writing,
understood in his sense of the word. Marion keeps the reduction
while rethinking it. The first reduction, Husserl's, involves the leading back of our relation to objects to consciousness, and the second
reduction, Heidegger's, is the passage from beings to being. Marion
proposes a third and more radical reduction: the self-giving of
givenness. Nothing can show itself unless it first gives itself. In harmony with this, Marion reformulates the subject of experience. No
longer is consciousness the transcendental subject that organizes
and gives meaning to experience. Instead, the subject is the *adonné*,
the gifted, the one who is given by what it receives.

* * *

Were we to arrange Marion's three triptychs into a single massive
triptych, the center would consist of *Reduction and Givenness*
(1989), *Being Given* (1997) and *In Excess* (2001). It has not always
seemed this way. Many readers have thought that theology, not phenomenology, indicates the true center of Marion's thought; and
some, most notably Dominique Janicaud (1937–2002), have
objected that his phenomenological meditations on the gift and

givenness are covert exercises in theology. Who or what is giving us phenomena? Why, since Marion is a Catholic, and since he explicitly meditates on Eucharistic presence, it must be God the Father. But this move is entirely illegitimate, Janicaud and others protest. Phenomenology cannot proceed without the reduction, and the first thing that falls to the reduction is transcendence. There can be a phenomenology of the sacred, since people experience the holy, but there cannot be a phenomenology of God because no one can have direct experience of the deity. In short, there is no way in which God can be revealed as the one who gives.

Far from disagreeing with these objections, Marion endorses them but holds that they fail to identify a fault in his work. One part of that work, he says, has been to distinguish as clearly as possible between phenomenology and revealed theology. He is right to insist on this, although it is easy to see how even sympathetic readers have misread him on precisely this issue. Some readers are distracted by the symmetry of Marion's program as a whole. He seeks to devise a theology that is without metaphysics, and he also develops a phenomenology that is without metaphysics. Incautious readers make the hasty induction that the phenomenology and the theology are the same thing. They are not: the theology indicates a God without being while the phenomenology secures a self without being and seeks to consider God only as a possibility. Yet there is a reason why people make the hasty induction, and it turns on *God Without Being* (1982), which, at least in the English-speaking world, is still the best known of Marion's books.

Anyone who reads *God Without Being* at all closely will notice a division in the book. The first five chapters explicate the difference between the idol and the icon in phenomenological terms, while also quietly presenting the philosophy of religion by way of the idol and the icon: metaphysics is tied to idolatry (it locks up God in concepts) while phenomenology, when properly understood, is oriented to the icon (it lets God be God). The final two chapters, which are given a separate heading, 'Hors-Texte', develop a theological meditation on the gift of presence. The subtitle 'Hors-Texte' is anything but innocent. It surely refers to Derrida's lapidary remark in *Of Grammatology* (1967), *il n'y a pas de hors-texte* (there is no *hors-texte*, or there is nothing outside the text). And just as surely those final two chapters suggest, 'There *is* something outside the text, namely the divine Word'. *Dieu sans l'être*: the French title drops two hints about the book's meaning to its readers that no English translation can capture. First, note the elided pronoun *l*: the book is about God when he is not being God, when he does not have to play the role that metaphysics has assigned to him. And second, *l'être* sounds just like *lettres*: the book is about God outside the text; it is about the eternal Word, not just words. (Derrida would agree in principle with the first, and would shrug a little impatiently when hearing the second: how can the Word, or anything, be discussed, he would ask, without difference?)

Phenomenology *and* theology: *God Without Being* does not seek to think the relation between the two, and it could be said that it takes Marion fifteen years, from *God without Being* (1982) until *Being Given* (1997), to overcome the rift in his earlier study. The later work attempts to think revelation from a strictly phenomenological perspective. Revelation, here, is not a gift from God the Father. That is a proposition that can be affirmed only by someone who has explicitly made an act of faith, and one that Marion, as a practicing Catholic, strongly affirms. Yet especially in his later work he wishes to do phenomenology, not theology, and to that end he develops a phenomenology of revelation. He does so by way of what he calls the saturated phenomenon, a notion that he takes pains to explicate in *Being Given* and *In Excess*.

When he was justifying the notion of religion without religion, Derrida cited Marion as someone whose work falls into that notion. Marion agrees: his phenomenology, though not his theology, can indeed be considered in that way. Revealed theology begins by thinking in faith that certain events occurred, and that these events have decisive significance for our redemption. Phenomenology, however, considers only the *possibility* of those events; it is concerned that those events can be thought, regardless of whether or not they actually took place. The point is not to establish a set of conditions that even God must respect if he is to reveal himself to us. That would be metaphysics at its very worst. Marion's task is to free revelation from such conditions, to let it be given in its own ways. If the theologian thinks of God's revelation as a gift, Marion wishes to contemplate the gift by way of givenness.

To think a phenomenon within metaphysics, Marion tells us, is to take it as poor in intuition. Now it would be a catastrophe to hear 'intuition', as used here, in the ordinary sense of the English word, namely, immediate insight. Marion employs the word in a technical way, as a translation of Husserl's German words *Anschaaung* and *Intuition*, and it might be better rendered as 'awareness'. Consider

Kant as the exemplary philosopher of thinking phenomena within metaphysics. He does so by using the categories of the understanding, as developed in his *Critique of Pure Reason* (1781; second edition, 1787). These categories constrain how we regard phenomena, and consequently what we can experience. They fall into four groups: Quantity, Quality, Relation and Modality. Kant takes as normative those phenomena that fall within my intentional horizon. I can aim at them (they have the quantity of unity, say), I can bear them (they have the quality of limitation, for instance), they fall within a horizon (they appear in a relation of cause and effect, for example), and I can gaze upon them (they have the modality of possibility, necessity or existence).

Quite exceptional in Kant's philosophical world would be a saturated phenomenon, namely one that I cannot aim at, or that dazzles me, or that imposes itself as absolute, or that cannot be gazed upon. What sort of thing is being talked about here? It is more ordinary than you might think at first. The Battle of Waterloo (1815) is a saturated phenomenon, Marion tells us: no one who was there – not even the Duke of Wellington or Napoléon or von Blücher – had an intentional rapport with the entire event. What we so blithely call '*the* Battle of Waterloo' was saturated with intuition; no one could break it down to a few things that could be identified and watched. In a different way, a painting by the American artist Mark Rothko (1903–70) is saturated with intuition: it conceals what is essential from my sight. My flesh is a saturated phenomenon, Marion adds: my pain and pleasure do not appear in your horizon. And so is your face: I endure your gaze when you summon me to help you, and it remains essentially invisible, even when I am staring into your eyes.

Only a phenomenology that has freed itself from metaphysics can think of a phenomenon saturated in intuition as normative. Consequently, only a non-metaphysical phenomenology, like the one that Marion believes himself to have devised, can make sense of the possibility of a phenomenon that is saturated in all four ways: it cannot be aimed at, it dazzles, it depends on no horizon, and cannot be gazed upon. This fourfold saturation is revelation, and in *Being Given* Marion devotes several beautiful pages to Christ as the revelation of God. Just because revelation is a possibility in a phenomenology that isn't metaphysical does not mean that Marion has smuggled theology into his philosophy. Phenomenology can bring you to the very brink of faith, but it cannot constrain you to make an act of faith. It is, if you like, a new way of describing what theologians call the *praeambula fidei*, the things we have to know before an act of faith can be made. One difference between Marion's phenomenology and Kant's is that revelation makes sense as a possibility. It is not relegated to the borders of religion neatly conceived as a rational project.

What shows itself first gives itself: such is Marion's understanding of the reduction. It solicits two questions. The first is who or what does the giving. Marion's answer: there is *no* giver, and that guarantees that the gift is pure. (There would be other ways: no gift and no one to give it to.) Brushing aside a swarm of questions about this claim, I pose the second question: To whom does it give itself? Not to the human subject, that is for sure. Marion agrees with all those postmodernists who object to the subject as Descartes and Kant have bequeathed it to us. There is no point, though, in trying to liquidate the subject, or whittling it down to something very small, no more than a place from which one speaks, or construing it as an effect of standing before venerable institutions such as Family, Government and Law. All those postmodern critiques of the subject fail, Marion argues, because the subject is no sooner repressed than it returns in another guise. The more effective task is to contest the originality of the subject, and we can best do that by proving that there is something prior to it. This is what Marion calls *l'adonné*, the gifted.

The first reduction, Husserl's, consisted of leading the subject back to his or her consciousness as constituting the meaning of experience in terms of an intentional horizon. It is this transcendental subject that Marion wishes to wrest from its position as absolutely resolute and self-regulating. The second reduction, Heidegger's, was a passage from beings to being, and it discloses *Dasein* as attuned to being. Even *Dasein*, 'being there', is too much of a subject, Marion thinks: it maintains a privileged position with respect to being and world. In the third reduction, Marion's, the 'me' is passively constituted by what gives itself. The subject must acknowledge that it comes after the gifted. Unlike the subject, the gifted cannot claim to master events. He or she must accept that phenomena are unforeseeable, that he or she has only a partial sense of the whole and is the recipient of meaning and not its bold constructor. The gifted has been called by givenness before an 'I' could be formed, before a response was even possible. Yet it is only in responding to that anonymous call, saying 'Here I am', that the gifted appears.

* * *

Theologians are sometimes puzzled by Marion's phenomenology. Why does he think that a revelation, considered as a saturation of saturation, has a connection with the Christian God? If you are dazzled by the saturation of saturation, it might be God revealing himself or it might be something else entirely, even something indifferent or malign. Also, why go to all the trouble of establishing the priority of givenness, people wonder, when you can directly turn to the New Testament and read that divine love has always and already called us out of selfhood. Since Marion is Catholic, he believes that Jesus Christ is the revealed Son of God. So what use can there be in elaborating a phenomenology that addresses the *possibility* of revelation?

John Milbank is a philosophical theologian who specializes in modern European thought, and is therefore finely aware of debates in phenomenology and their stakes for theology. He is one of Marion's most persistent partners in debate, although, interestingly enough, he does not base his disagreements with Marion on the two things that I have just mentioned. His concern is with Marion's account of the gift. Before getting to that, though, let's take a moment or two to situate Milbank in contemporary debate. We can say, first of all, that he is an Anglo-Catholic theologian. He belongs to that small group in the Church of England who look neither to the Reformation nor to the Counter-Reformation. Like John Henry Newman (1801–90) in the years before his conversion to the Catholic faith, Milbank treads the *via media*. Equally important is that Milbank is deeply English in his sensibility. Although he teaches in the United States and is intellectually attuned to modern European thought, he is drawn to an English interpretation of Christendom of which only a remnant remains. He dreams of a peaceful country, of towns with harmonious social differences, a community alive and well underneath the level of the State: a green and pleasant land, perhaps. He knows that in some respects it has passed forever, yet he compensates for his lost dream with a vigorous vision. Perhaps the remnant can be revived in postmodern times, and in a way that is less stuffy and more venturesome than before.

In theology, this emphasis on social harmony is Augustinian. And indeed Milbank's brief was first summed up as postmodern critical Augustinianism. His St Augustine is the author of *On Music* and *The City of God*, rather than the prayerful and tearful penitent of the *Confessions* who has attracted Derrida and Lyotard. Yet Milbank changed his brief to the snappier title of radical orthodoxy, and it is worth taking a moment or two to clarify what these two words mean. First, the theology to be affirmed is orthodox: it is grounded in the Nicene Creed (325). Second, it is radical; and this has several relevant senses. To begin with, it goes back to the roots of the Christian tradition, not only to the Nicene Creed but also to the Church Fathers, especially those most influenced by Plato. Also, Milbank's theology seeks to be radical in that it addresses postmodern life in all its manifestations: in the church and in the streets, in the city and in the flesh, in its nihilism and in its pluralism. This address is radical in that it involves a stinging criticism of modernity (presented as a stripped-down version of von Balthasar's account, with some additional demonizing of Duns Scotus) and a half-turn back to the premodern, especially to St Augustine. The modern secular consensus that the public sphere is rational, and should be expanded without limit because it *is* rational, is to be contested on the ground that it was once religious or at least quasi-religious. Once there was thorough social participation, and perhaps there can be again. A deep continuity runs between premodernity and postmodernity, Milbank thinks, although he is quick to point out the banality of the postmodernist default response: if in doubt, differ. The premodern cannot be retrieved but, once properly understood, can be inserted into postmodern thought. Finally, radical orthodoxy is radical in that it endorses socialism: not because it offers a rational theory of the state but because it preaches justice. Milbank's Marx is a prophet, not an economist.

Radical Orthodoxy is also the name of a movement, the other chief figures being Catherine Pickstock and Graham Ward, and while this group has served as a platform for Milbank it has also distracted people from what is original and important in his work. Just as Karl Barth attracted Barthians, so in his own way Milbank magnetizes former students and a former teacher, Rowan Williams, the current Archbishop of Canterbury. The movement has generated more heat than light and, like most intellectual fashions, has a good many adherents who have simply seen, heard, and then bought the show bag of ideas. Milbank is an interesting theologian; radical orthodoxy is a bore. It would be nice if a distinction could be drawn as sharply as that, but unfortunately it can't. In the interval between *Theology and Social Theory* (1990) and *The Word Made*

Strange (1997) Milbank became less interested in narrative theology and more taken with ontology. Partly this is the dynamic of his project (narrative making is of course a sort of participation) and partly it is the influence of Pickstock. The association with his student has led to Milbank's weakest moments: the co-authored book *Truth in Aquinas* (2001), for instance. Already drawn to Christian Platonism, which both then and now reduces Christianity to a modification of a philosophy, Milbank was led further down that path. One other thing should be said about radical orthodoxy as a movement. Although it excoriates many aspects of modernity, it remains profoundly modern in its program of transforming Christ into a speculative idea. Christianity, for the radically orthodox, exists at the level of theory.

Theology can be intellectually sophisticated and still remain effective pastorally. Regardless of how one rates his theological anthropology, Rahner was a surefooted pastoral theologian. Similarly, von Balthasar's theology is independent in its philosophical stances, and yet it addresses Christian existence at the level of the parish and the individual. His many popular works bear testimony to that. Few people would say the same of radical orthodoxy. The primary focus of the group has been on how theology can position other discourses, not on how Christ can transform your life and mine. Yet this criticism can, and has, been made too bluntly. It must be recognized that Christianity has tolerated, even encouraged, diverse interpretations of its central message, and has allowed that message to have different vehicles. Besides, radical orthodoxy ultimately offers itself as a vision of Christian social practice. It does so partly by way of rejecting the idea of an absolute sovereign power that is needed to arbitrate between moral and religious disputes. And it does so partly by way of arguments with Heidegger, Lévinas, Derrida and Marion: the most important philosophers of the gift.

* * *

Anyone who reads the *Confessions* (*c.*400) knows that St Augustine was fascinated by Manicheanism, the religious philosophy that argued that matter was intrinsically evil, and that he wrestled with it long after he had converted to the Catholic faith. Fewer people know that the saint spent considerable time and energy combating the Donatists, a powerful rival to the Catholic Church in fourth-century northern Africa. The church took its name from Donatus, the schismatic bishop of Carthage. Charismatic and purist in their leanings, the Donatists held that sacraments were valid only when the Holy Spirit was present in a priest. They resisted all attempts to let Christianity exist peacefully with the Roman Empire, and some of them actively sought the gift of death as martyrs.

We might see Milbank as a postmodern St Augustine trying to counter a new group of Donatists, this time the philosophers of *le don*, the gift. For all their disagreements Heidegger and Lévinas, Derrida and Marion, all figure the gift in terms of asymmetry. Heidegger considers being as gift, while Lévinas launches an ethics based on giving without expectation of return. Can a gift be given? That is Derrida's question in *Given Time I* (1991), and since it is a question that animates Marion and Milbank we need to ponder it. On the face of it, the answer would appear to be no. If I give you a present and you give me another in return, then there has really been no act of giving: we have only entered a circuit of exchange. No sooner do I receive something from you (a present in return or a smile) than the gift has been annulled. Even a frown will abolish the gift character of what I have given you, since it entitles me to feel superior to someone who has been so rude. Yet the problem of the gift, as Derrida points out, cannot be resolved by a direct appeal to asymmetry. Even if I merely form the intention of giving you something, I have entered into the world of exchange. The gift is obliterated just by the fact that it has appeared as a gift in my consciousness. For a gift to be given, all calculations and all intentions with respect to it, would have to be evaded by both parties. That is, we could never *know* if a gift has been given or received. If there is such a thing as the gift, it cannot be discussed in the language of philosophy, which of course includes phenomenology.

Those who think that Lévinas is a little extreme in thinking of ethics by way of a unilateral gift of assistance, and that Derrida is being far too purist about gifts, will perhaps see the point of my allusion to the Donatists. Why does Milbank oppose his older contemporaries? Because he maintains that gifts can and should be given. The gift should not be purified out of existence. Rather, gift giving is an essential part of human activity, as anthropologists have long realized; it is one of the most important things that holds society together. We have Bronislaw Malinowski (1884–1942) and Marcel Mauss (1872–1950) to thank for showing us early in the twentieth century that the oldest societies rely on gift exchange, not barter. More than being an index of sociality, though, purified exchange is a fundamentally Christian activity. The gospel enjoins us to avoid lawsuits and to practice mutual forgiveness: 'if thy brother shall trespass against thee, go and tell him his fault between thee and him alone: if he shall hear thee, thou has gained a brother' (Matt. 18:15). We are not to abide by the adage *du ut des*, give in order to receive, but we are to be hospitable and forgiving. In short, Christianity extols us not to avoid giving gifts but rather to purify the practice of gift exchange. That is the sign of divine love, *agape*.

If we look back to the middle ages, Milbank suggests, we can see how thoroughly society was organized by mutual exchange. It was part of a general structure of participation, the intellectual basis of which can be traced back to St Augustine and, in particular, to his Neoplatonic milieu. The City of God, as St Augustine conceived it, is a mobile community whose members exist in harmony with one another and with God. All their actions presume the absolute priority of the transcendent divine and the need to be oriented towards it. To perform a good action is not only to do something here and now but also to participate in the being of God. The contingency and ordinariness of my daily life are not cancelled or despised but transformed: in helping my friend or neighbor I remain myself while also becoming more like Christ. In this vision of society, evil is not an alternate principle of reality to be finally overcome; it is lack of being because it does not participate in God. Indeed, for Milbank metaphysical dualisms tend to be dangerous and are to be resisted in the interests of peace. Modernity is irreducibly dualist, he thinks, and nowhere is this more apparent than in the philosophy of Descartes. Indeed, the asymmetry of the gift originates in the seventeenth century and not in the twentieth. Doubtless the conditions for modernity break out earlier, in Duns Scotus and Suárez, but it is in Descartes that it gains a firm foothold in his notion of the human subject that freezes the flux of experience and alienates the mind from the body.

Reciprocal gift giving is important for Milbank both as a social practice and as a dimension of theology. The two cannot properly be distinguished because the former is a ground of the latter (Christendom) as well as being its pastoral extension. Let us begin by looking at theology, however. That Descartes is responsible for the invention of the human subject is a commonplace in the history of philosophy. That the birth of the subject occurs only with the death of the soul is also a familiar burden in histories of theology.

Milbank's thesis, however, is quite original. It is this. The Cartesian subject is co-ordinate with the asymmetry of gift giving while the soul is co-ordinate with reciprocity. And here is his proposal: we should abandon the subject and affirm a new understanding of the soul. By way of doing this, Milbank seeks to uncover the Cartesian assumptions of Heidegger, Lévinas, Derrida and Marion. From his viewpoint, they are insufficiently postmodern in their thought precisely because they follow Descartes in affirming the asymmetry of gift giving.

Is Lévinas, the very thinker who denies the priority of the self and declares in favor of the other person, a Cartesian? Surely not. Of course, we know that he borrows Descartes's insight that the infinite precedes the finite in human consciousness; but that does not make him Cartesian in the sense of affirming the priority of the *cogito* and the system of representation that is consequent on it. Yet Milbank insists that Lévinas develops an inverted Cartesianism, one that verges on the very Manicheanism from which St Augustine saved himself. For Descartes, it is the 'I' that forms the basis of understanding, indeed of all philosophy, while for Lévinas it is the other person. The model remains Cartesian, Milbank thinks; it is just that the ground has changed from self to other. And yet the ground has not really changed at all, for the other can be no more than a projection of the 'I'. Were Lévinas's ethics based on representation, this might be so. But it is not. He develops an ethics of responsibility that is independent of any system of representation, Cartesian or otherwise. That is one reason why he takes such pains to develop a notion of the immemorial past. A woman knocks on my door, asking for help. I am always and already responsible for her, Lévinas argues, even though I have never contracted to answer for her and have played no role whatsoever in bringing her to the sorry condition in which I now find her. She comes to me from a past that has never been present for me. Lévinas's ethics turns, then, on finding a bestowal of meaning that is ethical, not epistemological.

We will escape modernity's claims on us, Milbank thinks, only if we retrieve and rework a form of reciprocity. We must rethink ourselves as souls rather than subjects. To do this is not to reintroduce a metaphysical dualism. On the contrary, for St Augustine the soul is the form of the body, not an interior theater of consciousness. Today, we need to associate soul and body again, to recognize that consciousness is prior to the division of subject and object, and in doing so to gain a better grasp of event and time. To affirm reciprocity, though, does not mire us in metaphysics, as so many of the postmodernists suspect. And in fact a strict reciprocity of *quid pro quo* is not what Milbank has in mind these days. To be sure, at first he urged us to purify gift exchange. Now, though, he affirms asymmetrical reciprocity. I do not give to you, and then you give to me, in a closed circle. A better image is available: we are linked in an endless spiral of giving and receiving. Apart from the image of the spiral, the correction of Lévinas is exactly the one proposed by Blanchot in 'The Relation of the Third Kind' (1962), as the dialogue is titled in *The Infinite Conversation* (1969). Instead of arguing against the postmodernists, Milbank seems to have adopted one of their positions.

In self-defense Milbank would argue that he takes his inspiration from another Maurice, namely Merleau-Ponty, specifically from 'The Intertwining', a chapter of his posthumous volume *The Visible and the Invisible* (1964). Now Milbank is not a follower of phenomenology: either it entrenches the modern subject, he thinks, or it comes up with a strange twist of the subject. Certainly it denies that there is a meaning in objects outside the self, a meaning that consists in their status as created beings. Yet in his late work Merleau-Ponty indicated an exit from phenomenology, and so his thought can be appropriated by radical orthodoxy. Perhaps so; and yet I am not convinced by Milbank's defense. His notion of asymmetrical reciprocity is a less sophisticated yet more detailed version of Blanchot's notion of double dissymmetry. The theologian who tries to save us from nihilism ends up close to the atheist who affirms nihilism. They stand close together, looking in opposite directions.

* * *

Milbank develops criticisms of Lévinas and Derrida, yet he is more intent on having Marion as a debating partner than either of the older philosophers. Partly this is because Marion is Christian: they dispute the same territory and, as Milbank says, Marion is always half right. Partly it is because he takes Marion to represent the most sophisticated, if unknowing, Cartesianism on offer: to demolish Marion's foundational phenomenology would be to overturn modernity at its most agile. Partly it is because Marion develops a phenomenology without metaphysics when, as Milbank puts it in the title of an essay, only theology overcomes metaphysics. And partly it is because he sees Marion's notion of givenness as the greatest danger to his own view. The heart of Milbank's theology is his vision of reciprocity, and he seeks to secure that social vision by theological means.

An admiring reader of Heidegger, Marion in *God without Being* nevertheless demurs over the German philosopher's thought of being as gift. On the contrary, the gift must be thought outside or beyond the distinction of being and beings. For Milbank, though, this distance between gift and the philosophical matrix of being and beings, does not take us even a step away from Descartes. It has the unfortunate consequence of rendering the gift quite vacuous. What, after all, is actually given on Marion's understanding? Only a call that comes from beyond being, one that makes no contribution to ethical existence. This is a very long way from the rich social life of gift and counter-gift that Milbank endorses. No gift without a structure of reciprocity already in place: that, in ten words, is Milbank's position. There is more than this at issue, though. The gift without being does not give us anything at all, and no relationship can be established on that basis. Only if there is a gift with content can a gift be given, since only then can it be received. What is offered and received, Milbank adds, is an infinite relationship. Again, the language recalls Blanchot: the distance between you and me is infinite because my responsibility for you is without bound. And again, Milbank would refuse the comparison. The founding gift is the Father's giving of the Holy Spirit. Since the Spirit is the relationship of the Father and the Son, it is being-in-relation that is primarily given to us. Marion also would wish to say that the gift is divine love. Milbank's point is that only a Trinitarian ontology can give us a solid sense of divine love as gift.

Only theology overcomes metaphysics: Milbank's bold formulation calls for comment. It would have seemed quite odd to the young St Augustine living in Milan and Cassiciacum, for whom no sharp distinction could be drawn between philosophy and theology. To be sure, a broken line runs between Christianity and Neoplatonism: the young St Augustine knew that very well. Yet he thought that Plato (approached by way of Cicero's dialogues) and Plotinus could supply an adequate vehicle for Christianity. The author of *The City of God*, completed when St Augustine was an old man, was far more circumspect: the eighth book offers a nuanced evaluation of Platonism, and notes that the Platonists do not worship God as they should. Yet Milbank is not endorsing either the young convert or the old bishop. He maintains that metaphysics, as Heidegger and his followers use the word (namely, as a discourse on presence), arises only with

Scotus and Suárez before spreading virulently in the philosophy of the subject and generating a nihilism that is almost identical with modernity and postmodernity. No phenomenology, however sophisticated it might be, can overcome modern metaphysics because its vanishing points are firmly set in the Cartesian *cogito*, regardless of whether or not their provenance is acknowledged. It is only theology, understood as a discourse on the soul rather than the subject, that can free us from metaphysics, and it does so by insisting on the asymmetric exchange being the condition of a gift being given.

Milbank's position is open to questions from many quarters. It is doubtful that metaphysics is a specifically modern phenomenon. What Derrida calls the metaphysics of presence can be found from Plato to Heidegger and beyond. It can certainly be found in the Neoplatonists, and while some of the Platonising Fathers saw no compelling reasons to distinguish Christianity from philosophy, we cannot say the same. The meaning of 'philosophy' has changed. No one today takes a major in Philosophy with a view to withdraw from the world in search of wisdom. We should be wary of reducing Christianity to a qualification of a philosophy, as happens when one tries to revive Christian Platonism today. We should be skeptical of a theology that declares everyone other than the radical orthodox group to be nihilists. And we should be wary of a theology that talks of mildly transforming what is given, rather than re-orienting it radically towards Christ. Although he admires both Barth and von Balthasar, Milbank takes little stock of their shared vision of a Christ who interrupts our ways and who calls us sharply to account.

Theology, for Milbank, is theory prosecuted by other means. It revolves less around Jesus Christ and the witness to him in the New Testament than around a speculative idea of the incarnate Logos. This notion of Christianity is pitted against other theories, chiefly of the subject and society, and the sheer verve of Milbank's intelligence and knowledge often suffices to make those other theories look bad. Very rarely does Milbank succeed in immanent critique: he is a practitioner of quick, not slow, reading. He makes no punctures in Derrida's account of the gift but presents an alternative view that proceeds as though Derrida's argument had been refuted. His case is always strongest when he provides a broader counter-history than is accepted by the person he pits himself against. That strength can be a weakness, however, for it leads him to make generalizations that are hard to sustain in the histories of philosophy and theology. And when he succeeds his triumph is the victory of

Christianity as a theory of social life over competing theories proposed by Émile Durkheim or Marx, Lévinas or Derrida.

Only the mean-spirited would deny that there is genuine strength in Milbank's vision of a Christendom that can be revived by a participatory ontology, a thoroughgoing notion of reciprocity and relation that is firmly based in the Trinity. He refuses the charge of nostalgia: the patristic and medieval notion of exchange is not to be recouped but reset in our postmodern times. How this is to occur in a world that has been profoundly changed by capitalist economics, a world that has been shrunk by globalization and fragmented by the breakdown of nation-states, is never made clear. Until those things are made plain, it is likely that he will be accused repeatedly of an Anglo-Catholic idealization of the medieval religious world. He refuses also the charge of economic thought: exchange, for him, is embedded in *agape*. That said, there is a radical difference between a theology built on a vision of a lost Christendom and a theology that answers to Christ as the sacrament of our redemption. The one prizes exchange. The other contemplates the excess that has been given to us, even in the depths of our inability to respond adequately to it, whether in adoration, art or ethical action.

further reading

Marion, Jean-Luc. *God without Being*, trans. Thomas A. Carlson, foreword by David Tracy. Chicago: University of Chicago Press, 1991.
——. *The Idol and Distance: Five Studies*, trans. and introd. Thomas A. Carlson. New York: Fordham University Press, 2001.
——. *Being Given: Toward a Phenomenology of Givenness*, trans. Jeffrey L. Kosky. Stanford: Stanford University Press, 2002.
——. *In Excess: Studies in Saturated Phenomena*, trans. Robyn Horner and Vincent Berraud. New York: Fordham University Press, 2002.
Milbank, John. 'Can a Gift be Given? Prolegomena to a Future Trinitarian Metaphysic', *Modern Theology* 11:1 (1995), 119–61.
——. 'Only Theology Overcomes Metaphysics', in *The Word Made Strange: Theology, Language, Culture*. Oxford: Basil Blackwell, 1997.
——. 'The Soul of Reciprocity', *Modern Theology* 17:3 (2001), 335–91 and 17:4 (2001), 485–507.

guides and another guide

'Oh, it's all you guides again. I haven't seen you since the first chapter. I suppose you've been sitting around that coffee shop. How come you're together? Made up at last, have we?'

'Actually, we've been following what you've been saying,' one of them says, the one with the badge that says, *les tours de postmodernisme.*

'And some of us don't like it one little bit,' another adds. 'For a start, you've taken away all our custom. There's hardly anyone left to guide around the postmodern world. We've taken to giving each other free tours!'

'Worse' (and now the one with the badge reading *Popular PoMo Tours* steps forward), 'you've given a very slanted account of the whole thing! Don't you realize that you've said hardly anything about Michel Foucault and Jacques Lacan, two of the most import-ant post-structuralists? And you've said very little about cultural studies ...'

'Well, I never promised anyone to give a tour of post-structuralism. Besides, isn't that what your friend over there does? Had I done that, I would have had quite a bit to say about Foucault and Lacan. I would have liked to have said a whole lot more about the political in postmodern times. I thought there would have been time to introduce Jean-Luc Nancy on community and Jürgen Habermas on communicative action. Even more, I wish I had had time to talk about psychoanalysis: not just Lacan but Julia Kristeva, Nicholas Abraham and Maria Torok. Once I imagined a whole side-trip on mourning in postmodernity, but I just ran out of time.'

'But you spent so much time on Blanchot, who is hardly a postmodernist ...'

'... and even on analytic philosophers like Quine and Davidson. How could you do *that*? Don't you remember that Quine objected when the University of Cambridge offered Derrida an honorary doctorate?'

'No one knows for sure where the border runs that separates modernity and postmodernity. I wanted to include Blanchot because he has had such an influence on Deleuze, Foucault and Derrida. You hear their names all the time, but Blanchot's, well, hardly ever. And he *is* important. The analytic philosophers? Yes, I think that the divide between European Philosophy and Analytic Philosophy is debilitating, driven more by ideologies than by intellectual serious-ness. People who read Heidegger carp about the cult of cleverness at Princeton, while folk devoted to David Lewis and Saul Kripke whine that Derrida doesn't write clearly. If that is really what years of study-ing philosophy amounts to, a curse on both your houses!'

'We don't talk about analytic philosophy so much any more. Nowadays it's *post*-analytic philosophy that's at the cutting edge.'

'Sorry, who are you? I don't recall meeting you at the coffee shop. Can you move your arm so I can see your badge? Thanks. Ah, now I see: *Critical Realism: Or, What Comes after Pomo*. I've heard about you guys. What are you up to?'

'Oh, we run tours on pragmatism and science, on human being and social structure and philosophy at large. We disagree among ourselves about all sorts of things, as philosophers usually do, but we agree that we are realists. Unlike some postmodernists, we don't think that the real is wholly constructed by language or ideology or metaphor or society. And we do our best to write clearly.'

'You sound just like my philosophy teachers a quarter of a century ago. So what's new?'

'I suppose a fair number of us agree that empiricism and positivism don't point the way ahead. We're probably less interested in the theory of knowledge than your teachers were, and the chances are that you'll find us talking a lot more about ontology than epistemology.'

'That's different. I remember many seminars about knowledge, and not many about being.'

'Can *I* say something? Thanks. Rather than talk about a book you didn't write, one that caves in to all that analytic philosophy, I'd like to know why you ignored all those women postmodernists, including all those in the third world.'

'You're right. I didn't say much about them. As I said a minute ago, I wanted to write about Kristeva and Torok, and had I written on postmodern feminism I would have had something to say about Michèle Le Doeuff. I wanted to say something about postmodern African philosophy as well. Remember, though, I did say that my focus would be postmodernism and religion.'

'And you said that you weren't a wholehearted admirer of post-modernism. I don't recall hearing much about the people whose work you *don't* like.'

'No? Oh well, a few slid by, now and then; maybe you didn't notice. I was going to say something about the L=A=N=G=U=A=G=E poets, but my good nature got the better of me. And as your friend said a moment ago, I didn't say anything about the lower end of cultural studies. Given the time, I would have preferred to talk about eco-criticism: postmodernism meets one of its limits in nature. I've tried to indicate that now and then, but it deserves an entire book. I can't hang around here talking, though. I've got a seminar to prepare for first thing tomorrow. See you. Ta ta. Goodnight, goodnight ...'

'Hold on, isn't that a high modernist gesture? Odd way to end your guide to postmodernism!'

'You're right. I guess I should end by saying something about fragments and shoring up my ruins and all that.'

'Now you're just being funny!'

'Hey, come back. No, no point. He's gone. Boy, I've had enough of that guy! So, what do you think, anyone want another drink? It's at least another half-hour before the next tour.'

further reading

López, José and Garry Potter, eds. *After Postmodernism: An Introduction to Critical Realism.* London: The Athlone Press, 2001.

Potter, Garry. *The Bet: Truth in Science, Literature and Everyday Knowledge.* Brookfield: Ashgate, 1999.

Woodisiss, Anthony. *Social Theory after Postmodernism.* London: Pluto Press, 1990.

glossary

allegory A narrative in which various events invite reconstruction as a second 'higher' narrative: John Bunyan's *Pilgrim's Progress*, for example. Allegoresis is an approach to interpretation, sometimes called the allegorical hermeneutic: the meaning of a text is constituted outside the text as another discourse. Among postmodern literary critics, it is Paul de Man who is chiefly associated with the figure of allegory. See his *Allegories of Reading* (1979).

alterity State of being other, even to the point of exceeding or interrupting being. Theologians talk of the alterity of God, while some postmodern ethicists, such as Blanchot and Lévinas, talk of the alterity of the other person.

canon From the Greek, *kanón*, 'measuring reed'. The collection of biblical writings deemed by the Church to be inspired. In literature, the canon of an author consists of his or her authentic writings. More generally, when literary critics talk of the canon of English literature they have in mind those works held to be authoritative. In our day, when the canon is under critique from various quarters, 'canonical criticism' is the passion of Harold Bloom. His sense of canonicity, it should be noted, is more marked by Hebraic rather than Greek understandings of canon formation. See his *The Western Canon* (1994).

cogito Latin, 'I think'. An abbreviation for René Descartes's remarkable rebuff to the encroachments of skepticism: *Cogito ergo sum* ('I think, therefore I am').

cyborg A human being that relies partly or wholly on a computer chip or another inorganic device in order to function.

deconstruction Adapted from Heidegger's word *Destruktion*, Derrida's 'deconstruction' indicates how a discourse has been put together from various earlier discourses and exposes any and all forced joins and smoothing over. Neither a methodology nor a series of theses, deconstruction cannot be isolated in order to be applied. Nor does it come simply from outside a text, as happens in traditional 'critique'. Rather, deconstruction has always and already commenced in the unevennesses of a text, and is glimpsed by the vigilant reader. The promise of deconstruction occurring in a text is affirmed by the reader, giving rise to a structure of double affirmation ('yes, yes'). Deconstructions occur in many ways, although several of Derrida's readings are regarded as exemplary. See his 'Plato's Pharmacy' in *Dissemination* (1981), *Of Grammatology* (1976), 'Signature Event Context' in *Margins of Philosophy* (1982) and *Of Spirit* (1989).

desire The word has been variously defined. For Lacan, desire is the difference between what the subject can fulfill and what can never be fulfilled. The subject requires the other person to give himself or herself fully, but this cannot be: desire will never be eliminated. For Deleuze and Guattari, desire as a lack is a symptom of the Oedipal family. I desire my mother's breast, for example, but since I cannot have it I must sublimate my desire by identifying with my father and seeking social success. If we step outside the Oedipal family, Deleuze and Guattari argue, we can think desire otherwise than as lack or need. The free flow of desire can be seen to precede any and all needs; it is pre-human. Life is a process of sheer becoming, which is logically distinct from the becoming of any given living thing. For Derrida also, desire is not essentially related to lack but is an affirmation.

différance A coinage of Derrida's that denotes an endless play of differing and deferring. It names both the condition of possibility for conceptuality and the condition of impossibility that any concept be self-identical. Différance does not form a firm ground and cannot be presented as such. See **transcendental**, especially 'quasi-transcendental'.

disaster The word derives from the Latin: *dis* (away from) + *aster* (star). For Blanchot, 'disaster' first of all names the Holocaust or Shoah. Yet it also denotes an old theme of his, the interruption of our lives by the Outside. This interruption has always and already occurred: we are unmoored in the universe, which, strictly speaking, should not be considered as unified, and there has been no star to herald a Messiah. We live in two spheres: in one we seek meaning, direction and unity; in another, we are consigned to non-meaning, no direction and the relation without relation. In that neutral sphere, we have been drawn towards the Outside. See **relation without relation** and **outside**.

empiricism The philosophy that argues that experience, not reason, is the origin of knowledge. Eighteenth-century thinkers John Locke, Bishop Berkeley and David Hume are the greatest of all empiricists, although the position is elaborated, with many lights, by John Stuart Mill in the nineteenth century and by any number of analytic philosophers in the twentieth century. The counterpart of Empiricism is known as Rationalism.

epistemology The theory of knowledge, especially its scope and its status. What can we know? Does knowledge differ from belief? What counts as knowledge? How reliable is our knowledge? These are the guiding questions of epistemology. The enemy of all epistemology is skepticism, which is kept at arm's length rather than refuted definitively by even the best philosophers. The most hostile of modern philosophers to epistemology is Heidegger who judges it to occlude the study of being.

epoché A word used by Husserl to denote the suspension of any natural attitude towards reality, e.g. 'common sense'. When you perform the *epoché*, you bracket all the theories on which we usually call to explain experience. See **phenomenology**, **intentionality** and **reduction**.

fragmentary Blanchot distinguishes the fragmentary from the fragment. The latter is a part of a whole; the former cannot be gathered into any sort of unity but rather exists in a relation without relation.

gnosticism A spiritual system that teaches the redemption of the spirit through knowledge, *gnosis*. Gnosticism braids together magic, mythology and philosophy, and posed a serious threat to Christianity in the first centuries of the Common Era. The 'gnostic symptom' can be detected in New Age spiritualities.

hermeneutics The theory of interpretation. 'Hermeneutics' derives from Hermes, the Greek god who communicated (and sometimes interpreted) messages sent from the Olympian gods to mortals.

The modern father of hermeneutics is Friedrich Schleiermacher (1768–1834) whose work was rethought and expanded by Wilhelm Dilthey (1833–1911). Heidegger developed several hermeneutical themes, and his former student, Hans-Georg Gadamer (1900–2002), became the principal exponent of philosophical hermeneutics.

humanism The word first appears in Renaissance Italy, and indicates thinking man in the contexts of nature and history. In the Renaissance, humanism was neither anti-religious in general nor anti-Christian in particular. For Jean-Paul Sartre, however, humanism denotes that existence precedes the essence of human beings: we do not have an essential nature. Sartrean humanism is incompatible with the existence of a God in whose sight we have fallen and must be redeemed. Heidegger argued that humanism is flawed because it seeks to think 'human being' as a rational animal, rather than as the sole being for whom being is a problem.

idealism The philosophical view that consciousness or mind is the irreducible ground of reality. Although the word is fairly recent, arising no later than the eighteenth century, the concept can be applied to earlier thinkers, indeed, to no less a philosopher than Plato. Yet Plato did not think that reality turned on consciousness or mind; rather, his view was that reality is apprehended by the intellect by way of grasping universals (i.e., whiteness rather than this white piece of chalk). After Plato, the greatest of all idealists is Hegel, although Fichte and Schelling are themselves formidable thinkers in that way.

intentionality A word that Husserl drew from medieval philosophy, by way of his teacher Franz Brentano, to denote an essential characteristic of consciousness, namely that all consciousness is always *of* something. Consciousness is not an inner state; it is an act. When you desire or perceive something, you make it part of your experience and relate to it as part of an intelligible whole. It is in performing the *epoché* and the phenomenological reduction that we can reflect on our intentional relations with the world. See **epoché**, **phenomenology** and **reduction**.

iterability One of Derrida's coinages, the word denotes a general condition: repetition leads to difference rather than a reinforcement of self-identity. On Derrida's analysis, no sign has ever had an original meaning; each sign – or, as he came to prefer, mark – has always and already been subject to the process of iterability. See **différance** and **trace**.

kabbalah The esoteric teachings of Judaism and, in particular, of Jewish mysticism. Unlike Christian mystics, the Kabbalists seldom sought union with God. Rather, their concern is characteristically with the interpretation of Torah. For the Kabbalists, Mosaic Law provides an inexhaustible world of symbols that, if read properly, will disclose the meaning of reality. In contemporary criticism, Harold Bloom has sought to revive Kabbalah as a model of strong reading (or, as he puts it, misreading). See his *Kabbalah and Criticism* (1984).

metaphysics For Aristotle, metaphysics is what, in the proper course of study, comes after physics. It is the study of being as being, and it addresses substance, potency and actuality, unity, as well as the prime mover. Late classical and medieval philosophers took the word to denote the study of those realities that are beyond the categories of nature. (See 'transcendentals' in **transcendental**.) With Kant, metaphysics comes to be considered as speculation on matters that cannot be settled by the natural sciences. Beginning in the 1930s, Heidegger announced the end of metaphysics: Nietzsche was the last philosopher to have made an original move in its sphere. The remaining task, he thought, was to overcome metaphysics; and we can do that by returning to its ground and venturing a new beginning. When we go back to the ground of metaphysics, we discover that it is constituted as onto-theology. Derrida coined the expression 'metaphysics of presence' and has attempted the deconstruction of that metaphysics. (See **deconstruction**, **onto-theology** and **presence**.)

moral law The moral law was formulated by Kant in the *Critique of Practical Reason*: 'So act that the maxim of your will could always hold at the same time as a principle establishing universal law.' A maxim, for Kant, is a 'subjective principle of volition'. For example, I might will a lie in order to save face, but if I refer my maxim to the moral law I will realize that I could not use it to establish a universal law. Much as I might wish to lie now, I do not think that *everyone* should be able to lie in order to save face.

nihilism The word derives from the Latin *nihil*, 'nothing', and was first associated with nineteenth-century Russian thinkers who held that traditional values should be tested by attacking them as vigorously as possible. Nietzsche took over the word, and for him it was a historical process – the devaluation of all values – that needed to be overcome. Heidegger develops a profound discussion of nihilism in his *Nietzsche*, while Blanchot meditates on the word in his *The Infinite Conversation*.

ontology From the Greek *to on*, 'that which is'. Ontology is the study of being. The word enters European philosophy as late as the seventeenth century, and is today mostly associated with the project of fundamental ontology in Heidegger's *Being and Time* (1927). Fundamental ontology is the analysis of *Dasein*, 'being there', with a view to posing the question about the meaning of being. Heidegger abandoned the project of fundamental ontology, but preserved the distinction between the ontic (to do with beings) and the ontological (to do with being). Among analytic philosophers, Quine has been the most interested in ontology, although he distances himself from Heidegger's understanding of the word. The word is also used in modern theology, whether or not it be influenced by Heidegger. A Trinitarian ontology, for example, is an account of the being of God considered in his triune nature as Father, Son and Holy Spirit.

onto-theology The word is first used by Kant to denote the attempt to think God through pure reason. He reckons this attempt a failure. Heidegger gives the word a new spin. Since ontology is the laying out of being and theiology is the saying of the highest being (Greek: *theion*), onto-theology (as it should be written) yields the structure of metaphysics: the gathering together of the general features of being and the study of the highest being. So metaphysics, on Heidegger's understanding, leagues beings to form a whole, the ground of which is being. Note that for Heidegger and for Derrida onto-theology arises in philosophy, not in religion, although some Christian theologians have promoted onto-theiological theses.

outside A word used by Maurice Blanchot, sometimes with a capital letter and sometimes not, to denote the unnerving sense of a space that approaches and interrupts the writer when engaged in literary work. With the approach of the outside, one is pulled towards the space of images and loses all sense of living in the first-person singular. Also see **relation without relation**.

phenomenology The name of a highly influential school of philosophy founded by Edmund Husserl and developed in original ways by Martin Heidegger, Emmanuel Lévinas, Maurice Merleau-Ponty, Jean-Paul Sartre, Michel Henry and Jean-Luc Marion, among others. Husserl's rallying cry was 'Back to the things themselves!' That is, he wished to describe phenomena as they present themselves to us, and not in terms of earlier philosophical assumptions and systems. See **epoché**, **intentionality** and **reduction**.

post-structuralism A broad spectrum of discourses that emerged in dialogues with and in departures from structuralism. The names most frequently cited in this regard are Deleuze, Derrida and Lacan, none of whom accepts the label. Some versions of feminism, psychoanalysis and Marxism are post-structuralist to lesser or greater extents.

pragmatism A philosophical movement centered in the United States of America, the main exponents of which are Charles Pierce, William James and John Dewey. It has been an influence on W.V.O. Quine, and its most eminent and consequent living representative is Richard Rorty. In contemporary debate, pragmatism evokes an attitude towards theory. A theory is justified, pragmatists hold, in terms of how well it meets our needs. Usefulness, rather than abstract truth, is the main criterion the pragmatist looks for in a discourse.

presence Heidegger talks of presence by way of several German words: *Der Augenblick, Anwesen, Anwesenheit, Gegenwart* and *Präsenz*. He is critical of any thought that freezes the coming of being into presence into a constant state of presentness. Derrida coins the expression 'metaphysics of presence', and grants it a considerable range of meaning: a subject's presence to itself; a being's presence in time; and the determination of being as presence. Also see **metaphysics**.

reduction Husserl describes several sorts of reduction, the most important of which are the eidetic and phenomenological (or transcendental) reductions. The eidetic reduction is performed when you grasp the principle of something, e.g., that all circles have 360 degrees. The phenomenological reduction is performed after the natural attitude has been bracketed. In performing the phenomenological reduction, you are led back to your experience as concretely embedded in the world. No longer is it presented to you as already explained by 'common sense' or 'natural science'. Also see **epoché** and **phenomenology**.

relation without relation Maurice Blanchot uses the expression to denote a way of being in relation that looks neither to dialectic nor to fusion. In the third relation, as he sometimes calls it, one is held together and apart by an infinite responsibility for the other person. The self and the other person cannot be formed into any sort of unity. Also see **outside**.

structuralism Impressed by the achievements of structural linguists such as Ferdinand de Saussure and Roman Jakobson, Claude Lévi-Strauss sought to revise anthropology along structural lines. Social structures, rather than particular beliefs and practices, were to be identified and analyzed. These consist of metaphorical and metonymic relations between social phenomena. Meaning occurs in the differential relations of cultural signs considered on the synchronic rather than the diachronic plane. (A synchronic analysis examines a language or a culture at one point in time; a diachronic analysis looks at the same phenomena over time.) Note that the relations are between signs, not between a sign and its referent: there is no one-to-one correspondence between a sign and what it names. Roland Barthes went through a structuralist phrase, while Derrida's early writings are a dialogue with structuralism and a departure from it. Also see **post-structuralism**.

subject Derived from the Latin *subiectum*, meaning 'that which is thrown under'. Usually with reference to Descartes and the tradition he spawned, 'subject' has been used to identify the human being, the *cogito* or 'I think'. Much of modern philosophy in Europe has been concerned with the subject, whether disembodied (as with Descartes) or embodied (as with Nietzsche and Merleau-Ponty). Hegel develops a memorable analysis of what happens when two subjects encounter one another in the Lord and Bondsman episode of the *Phenomenology of Mind*. Heidegger seeks to redescribe being human by way of *Dasein*, 'being there', rather than as subject.

talmud A massive body of commentary on the Torah, understood as both the Oral and Written Law given to Moses. It consists of the Mishnah, the first written account of the Oral Law, and the Gemara, a commentary on the Mishnah. Talmudic commentary includes both Halakhah (normative rulings) and Aggadah (guidance and stories that do not bear on normative rulings).

theology The study of God. Positive theologies attempt to understand the deity by way of what has been revealed to human beings, and try to talk of God in positive terms (e.g. 'God is One'). Negative theologies contest the appropriateness of positive predications of the deity: if God is transcendent, then divinity exceeds all the resources

of language. Negative theologies do not place special value on nega-
tions but rather use the syntax of neither-nor (e.g. 'God is neither
One nor Many'). Natural theologies attempt to approach God from
the natural world (by finding design, for example), while revealed
theologies seek to interpret God on the basis of the revealed word.
Non-metaphysical theologies venture to talk about God without
recourse to metaphysical categories (e.g. cause and effect) or, in
more recent decades, by way of the deconstruction of the metaphysics of presence. Trinitarian theologies expound the mystery of
the Christian God as triune, i.e., as Father, Son and Holy Spirit.

trace Although the word plays a role in thought as different as
Plotinus's and Freud's, and was introduced by Lévinas, it is best
known these days as part of Derrida's vocabulary. No absolutely singular item can present itself without exposing itself to the possibility
of repetition. Indeed, if there is no empirical repetition, the item is
nonetheless divided by dint of the possibility of this repetition. The
absolute character of its singularity is therefore withdrawn in its very
presentation, leaving only a trace of that absolute character.

transcendence In religion, transcendence refers to the aseity of
God, namely the belief that the deity derives *a se*, from itself, and
therefore cannot be deduced from either being or non-being. Ethical
transcendence consists in the claim that the other person cannot be
reduced to a correlative of my consciousness.

transcendental The word is drawn from Kant's critical philosophy
and widely used in phenomenology and post-phenomenological
thought. A transcendental condition is a condition of possibility.
Derrida talks of quasi-transcendental conditions, that is, conditions
of possibility that are at the same time conditions of impossibility.
For example, *la différance* is the condition of possibility for a text's
identity and the condition of impossibility for its self-identity.
Transcendentals are those predicates that apply to all real or possible
beings. For example, beauty, being, goodness, truth and unity can be
predicated of all beings regardless of the category to which they
belong or, in the case of God, of that which exceeds all categories.

bibliography

1. books recommended in the chapters

Adam, A.K.M., ed. *Postmodern Interpretations of the Bible: A Reader*. St Louis: Chalice Press, 2001.

Aichele, George, *et al. The Postmodern Bible*. New Haven: Yale University Press, 1995.

Baudrillard, Jean. *Selected Writings*, ed. and introd. Mark Poster. Stanford: Stanford University Press, 1988.

——. *The Gulf War Did Not Take Place*, trans. Paul Patton. Bloomington: Indiana University Press, 1995.

Bauman, Zygmunt. *Life in Fragments: Essays in Postmodern Morality*. Oxford: Basil Blackwell, 1995.

Benjamin, Walter. *The Arcades Project*, trans. Howard Eiland and Kevin McLaughlin. Cambridge: The Belknap Press of Harvard University Press, 1999.

Blanchot, Maurice. *The Writing of the Disaster*, trans. Ann Smock. Lincoln: University of Nebraska Press, 1986.

——. *The Infinite Conversation*, trans. and foreword Susan Hanson. Minneapolis: University of Minnesota Press, 1993.

——. *The Work of Fire*, trans. Charlotte Mandell. Stanford: Stanford University Press, 1995.

Bloom, Harold. *Ruin the Sacred Truths: Poetry and Belief from the Bible to the Present*. Cambridge: Harvard University Press, 1989.

Bové, Paul A., ed. *Early Postmodernism: Foundational Essays*. Durham: Duke University Press, 1995.

Caputo, John D. *The Prayers and Tears of Jacques Derrida: Religion without Religion*. Bloomington: Indiana University Press, 1997.

——, ed. *The Religious*. Oxford: Basil Blackwell, 2002.

—— and Michael J. Scanlon, eds. *God, the Gift and Postmodernism.* Bloomington: Indiana University Press, 1999.

Danto, Arthur. *Nietzsche as Philosopher.* New York: Macmillan, 1967.

Derrida, Jacques. *Specters of Marx: The State of the Debt, the Work of Mourning, and the New International,* trans. Peggy Kamuf, introd. Bernd Magnus and Stephen Cullenberg. London: Routledge, 1994.

——. *The Gift of Death,* trans. David Wills. Chicago: University of Chicago Press, 1995.

—— and Gianni Vattimo, eds. *Religion,* trans. Samuel Weber. Cambridge: Polity Press, 1998.

Eco, Umberto (with Richard Rorty, Jonathan Culler and Christine Brooke-Rose). *Interpretation and Overinterpretation,* ed. Stefan Collini. Cambridge: Cambridge University Press, 1992.

Fenves, Peter, ed. *Raising the Tone of Philosophy: Late Essays by Immanuel Kant, Transformative Critique by Jacques Derrida.* Baltimore: The Johns Hopkins University Press, 1993.

Fish, Stanley. *Doing What Comes Naturally: Change, Rhetoric, and the Practice of Theory in Literary and Legal Studies.* Oxford: Clarendon Press, 1989.

Foster, Hal, ed. *Anti-Aesthetic: Essays on Postmodern Culture.* Port Townsend: Bay Press, 1983.

Hart, Kevin. *The Trespass of the Sign: Deconstruction, Theology and Philosophy,* expanded edition. New York: Fordham University Press, 2000.

Jobling, David, *et al.,* eds. *The Postmodern Bible Reader.* Oxford: Basil Blackwell, 2001.

Kearney, Richard. *Dialogues with Contemporary Continental Thinkers: The Phenomenological Heritage.* Manchester: Manchester University Press, 1984.

Lacoue-Labarthe, Philippe and Jean-Luc Nancy. *The Literary Absolute: The Theory of Literature in German Romanticism,* trans., introd. and notes Philip Bernard and Cheryl Lester. Albany: State University of New York Press, 1988.

López, José and Garry Potter, eds. *After Postmodernism: An Introduction to Critical Realism.* London: The Athlone Press, 2001.

Lyotard, Jean-François. *The Postmodern Condition: A Report on Knowledge,* trans. Geoff Bennington and Brian Massumi, foreword Frederic Jameson. Minneapolis: The University of Minnesota Press, 1984.

——. *The Postmodern Explained to Children: Correspondence 1982–1985,* trans. and ed. Julian Pefanis and Morgan Thomas. Sydney: Power Publications, 1992.

Marion, Jean-Luc. *God without Being,* trans. Thomas A. Carlson, foreword David Tracy. Chicago: University of Chicago Press, 1991.

Marion, Jean-Luc. *The Idol and Distance: Five Studies*, trans. and introd. Thomas A. Carlson. New York: Fordham University Press, 2001.

——. *Being Given: Toward a Phenomenology of Givenness*, trans. Jeffrey L. Kosky. Stanford: Stanford University Press, 2002.

——. *In Excess: Studies in Saturated Phenomena*, trans. Robyn Horner and Vincent Berraud. New York: Fordham University Press, 2002.

Milbank, John. 'Can a Gift be Given? Prolegomena to a Future Trinitarian Metaphysic', *Modern Theology* 11:1 (1995), 119–61.

——. *The Word Made Strange: Theology, Language, Culture*. Oxford: Basil Blackwell, 1997.

——. 'The Soul of Reciprocity', *Modern Theology* 17:3 (2001), 335–91 and 17:4 (2001), 485–507.

Potter, Garry. *The Bet: Truth in Science, Literature and Everyday Knowledge*. Brookfield: Ashgate, 1999.

Prickett, Stephen, ed. *Reading the Text: Biblical Criticism and Theory*. Oxford: Basil Blackwell, 1991.

Quasha, George, ed. *The Station Hill Blanchot Reader*. Barrytown: Station Hill Press, 1999.

Rockmore, Tom and Beth J. Singer, eds. *Antifoundationalism Old and New*. Philadelphia: Temple University Press, 1992.

Rorty, Richard. *Contingency, Irony, and Solidarity*. Cambridge: Cambridge University Press, 1989.

Schwartz, Regina, ed. *The Book and the Text: The Bible and Literary Theory*. Oxford: Basil Blackwell, 1990.

Taylor, Mark C. *Erring: A Postmodern A/Theology*. Chicago: University of Chicago Press, 1984.

Venturi, Robert, Denise Scott Brown and Steven Izenour. *Learning from Las Vegas: The Forgotten Symbolism of Architectural Form*. Cambridge: MIT Press, 1972.

Westphal, Merold, ed. *Postmodern Philosophy and Christian Thought*. Bloomington: Indiana University Press, 1999.

Whitford, Margaret, ed. *The Irigaray Reader*. Oxford: Basil Blackwell, 1991.

Woodisiss, Anthony. *Social Theory after Postmodernism*. London: Pluto Press, 1990.

2. further reading

Bauman, Zygmunt. *Postmodernity and its Discontents*. New York: New York University Press, 1997.

Bertens, Hans. *The Idea of the Postmodern: A History*. London: Routledge, 1995.

Bloom, Harold. *The American Religion: The Emergence of the Post-Christian Nation*. New York: Simon and Schuster, 1992.

Caputo, John D. *Deconstruction in a Nutshell.* New York: Fordham
 University Press, 1997.
——. *On Religion.* London: Routledge, 2001.
—— and Mark Dooley and Michael J. Scanlon, eds. *Questioning God.*
 Bloomington: Indiana University Press, 2001.
Chauvet, Louis-Marie. *Symbol and Sacrament: A Sacramental
 Reinterpretation of Christian Existence,* trans. Patrick Madigan, SJ and
 Madeleine Beaumont. Collegeville: The Liturgical Press, 1995.
De Certeau, Michel. *The Mystic Fable,* trans. Michael B. Smith. Chicago:
 University of Chicago Press, 1992.
Derrida, Jacques. *Given Time I: Counterfeit Money,* trans. Peggy Kamuf.
 Chicago: The University of Chicago Press, 1992.
Florensky, Pavel. *The Pillar and Ground of the Truth,* trans. Boris Jakim,
 intro. Richard F. Gustafson. Princeton: Princeton University Press,
 1997.
Hart, Kevin. *The Dark Gaze: Maurice Blanchot and the Sacred.* Chicago: The
 University of Chicago Press, 2004.
—— and Yvonne Sherwood, eds. *Other Testaments: Derrida and Religion.*
 London: Routledge, 2004.
Hartman, Geoffrey. *Scars of the Spirit: The Struggle Against Inauthenticity.*
 New York: Palgrave, 2002.
Holland, Michael, ed. *The Blanchot Reader.* Oxford: Basil Blackwell, 1995.
Horner, Robyn. *Rethinking God as Gift: Marion, Derrida, and the Limits
 of Phenomenology.* New York: Fordham University Press, 2001.
Janicaud, Dominique, *et al. Phenomenology and the 'Theological Turn': The
 French Debate,* trans. Bernard G. Prusak *et al.* New York: Fordham
 University Press, 2000.
Lévinas, Emmanuel. *Ethics and Infinity: Conversations with Philippe Nemo,*
 trans. Richard A. Cohen. Pittsburgh: Duquesne University Press, 1985.
——. *Is it Righteous to Be? Interviews with Emmanuel Lévinas,* ed. Jill
 Robbins. Stanford: Stanford University Press, 2001.
Marion, Jean-Luc. *On Descartes' Metaphysical Prism,* trans. Jeffrey
 L. Kosky. Chicago: The University of Chicago Press, 1999.
Milbank, John. *Theology and Social Theory: Beyond Secular Reason.* Oxford:
 Basil Blackwell, 1990.
——. *Being Reconciled: Ontology and Pardon.* London: Routledge, 2003.
Nancy, Jean-Luc. *The Inoperative Community,* ed. Peter Connor, trans.
 Peter Connor *et al.* Minneapolis: University of Minnesota Press, 1991.
——. *The Sense of the World,* trans. and foreword Jeffrey S. Librett.
 Minneapolis: University of Minnesota Press, 1997.
Norris, Christopher. *Uncritical Theory: Postmodernism, Intellectuals and the
 Gulf War.* Amherst: University of Massachusetts Press, 1992.
Rosenzweig, Franz. *The Star of Redemption,* trans. William W. Hallo.
 Notre Dame: University of Notre Dame Press, 1985.

Vattimo, Gianni. *The Transparent Society*, trans. David Webb. Baltimore: The Johns Hopkins University Press, 1992.

——. *Belief*, trans. Luca D'Isanto and David Webb. Stanford: Stanford University Press, 1999.

Von Balthasar, Hans Urs. *The Glory of the Lord: A Theological Aesthetics*, V: *The Realm of Metaphysics in the Modern Age*, trans. Oliver Davies *et al.*, ed. Brian McNeil and John Riches. Edinburgh: T. and T. Clark, 1991.

websites

Barthes, Roland
http://we.got.net/~tuttle/

Bataille, Georges
http://www.kirjasto.sci.fi/bataille.htm

Baudrillard, Jean
http://www.uta.edu/english/apt/collab/baudweb.html

Bauman, Zygmunt
http://www.shef.ac.uk/uni/academic/N-Q/perc/bauman.pdf

Beckett, Samuel
http://home.sprintmail.com/~lifeform/Beck_Links.html

Benjamin, Walter
http://home.cwru.edu/~ngb2/Authors/Benjamin.html

Blanchot, Maurice
http://lists.village.virginia.edu/~spoons/blanchot/blanchot_mainpage.htm

Borges, Jorge Luis
http://www.kirjasto.sci.fi/jlborges.htm

Burroughs, William
http://www.levity.com/corduroy/burroughs.htm

Calvino, Italo
http://www.emory.edu/EDUCATION/mfp/cal.html

Celan, Paul
http://polyglot.lss.wisc.edu/german/celan/biblio/

Cixous, Hélène
http://www.erraticimpact.com/~feminism/html/women_cixous.htm

Davidson, Donald
http://www.utm.edu/research/iep/d/davidson.htm

Deleuze, Gilles
http://www.uta.edu/english/apt/d&g/d&gweb.html

DeLillo, Don
http://perival.com/delillo/delillo.html

De Man, Paul
http://sun3.lib.uci.edu/~scctr/Wellek/deman/

Derrida, Jacques
http://www.hydra.umn.edu/derrida/

Eco, Umberto
http://www.levity.com/corduroy/eco.htm

Eisenman, Peter
http://www.iit.edu/departments/pr/arch.comp/eisenman.html

Fish, Stanley
http://www.mv.helsinki.fi/home/kniemela/fish.htm

Foucault, Michel
http://www.csun.edu/~hfspc002/foucault.home.html

Freud, Sigmund
http://www.utm.edu/research/iep/f/freud.htm

Habermas, Jürgen
http://www.habermasonline.org/

Hegel, G.W.F.
http://plato.stanford.edu/entries/hegel/

Heidegger, Martin
http://www.utm.edu/research/iep/h/heidegge.htm

Husserl, Edmund
http://www.utm.edu/research/iep/h/husserl.htm

Irigaray, Luce
http://www.cddc.vt.edu/feminism/irigaray.html

Joyce, James
http://www.cohums.ohio-state.edu/english/organizations/ijjf/jrc/default.htm

Kafka, Franz
http://www.pitt.edu/~kafka/links.html

Kristeva, Julia
http://www.pdcnet.org/kristeva.html

Lacan, Jacques
http://lacan.com/

Lévinas, Emmanuel
http://home.pacbell.net/atterton/levinas/

Lyotard, Jean-François
http://lists.village.virginia.edu/~spoons/lyotard-bib.html

Mallarmé, Stéphane
http://www.studiocleo.com/librarie/mallarme/mallarme.html

Marion, Jean-Luc
http://www.calvin.edu/academic/philosophy/smith/marion.htm

Milbank, John
http://www.calvin.edu/~jks4/ro/

Nietzsche, Friedrich
http://plato.stanford.edu/entries/nietzsche/

Pynchon, Thomas
http://www.hyperarts.com/pynchon/

Quine, Willard van Orman
http://www.wvquine.org/

Rahner, Karl
http://www.theo.mu.edu/krs/

Robbe-Grillet, Alain
http://www.halfaya.org/robbegrillet/

Rorty, Richard
http://www.stanford.edu/~rrorty/

Saussure, Ferdinand de
http://www.marxists.org/reference/subject/philosophy/works/fr/saussure.htm

Sellars, Wilfred
http://plato.stanford.edu/entries/sellars/

Von Balthasar, Hans Urs
http://www.catechesis.net/vonbalthasar/

Wittgenstein, Ludwig
http://www.utm.edu/research/iep/w/wittgens.htm

index of names

index of subjects

178

Great Figures in History

Einstein

Albert Einstein

Y. kids
www.myykids.com

Great Figures in History

Einstein

ISBN: 978-981-054944-2
Printed and bound in the Republic of Korea.

How to contact us
E-mail: feedback@myykids.com

Credits
Adaptation & Art: SAM (Special Academic Manga)
Production Manager: Suzie Lee
Editorial Services: Publication Services, Inc.
Developmental Editor: Rachel Lake, Publication Services, Inc.
Editorial Manager: Lorie Donovan, Publication Services, Inc.
Book Designer: SAM (Special Academic Manga)
Cover Designer: Litmus
Production Control: Jay Won, Misook Kim